THE SOCIAL MESSAGE
OF JESUS

By
JOHN H. MONTGOMERY

Professor Religious Education
University Southern California

Introduction by
SHAILER MATHEWS

WIPF & STOCK · Eugene, Oregon

Wipf and Stock Publishers
199 W 8th Ave, Suite 3
Eugene, OR 97401

The Social Message of Jesus
By Montgomery, John H. and Mathews, Shailer
Softcover ISBN-13: 978-1-7252-9675-6
Hardcover ISBN-13: 978-1-7252-9674-9
eBook ISBN-13: 978-1-7252-9676-3
Publication date 1/7/2021
Previously published by The Abingdon Press, 1923

This edition is a scanned facsimile of
the original edition published in 1923.

CONTENTS

	PAGE
INTRODUCTION	7
PREFACE	9

PART ONE

THE SOCIAL IMPLICATIONS OF THE GOSPEL

CHAPTER

I. THE SOCIAL QUESTION.......................... 13

Definition—A modern problem, truly significant of this age—Radical in its nature, examining the very foundations of society—A moral issue growing out of the recognition of the social need.

II. THE MASTER'S APPRAISAL OF LIFE.............. 22

What is an authority?—Jesus experienced life extensively—He observed accurately and with keen penetration—He occupied a detached position with relation to life—His view was authoritative and divine—It is worth while to heed his appraisal.

III. THE WORTH OF A MAN......................... 32

Two ways of approaching social problems; as affecting individuals; considering the mass—Both are needed, but Jesus uses mainly the former—Jesus' high appreciation of men evidenced by his willingness to talk to individuals—The individualism of his parables and teachings—A high regard for personality, the "hall mark" of Christianity.

IV. BROTHERHOOD................................. 42

Fellowship and the solidarity of the human family— Jesus would go to great lengths to preserve solidarity—He identifies himself with the race—Social conscience is implied—The physical, mental, and moral interrelations—Certain tendencies exclusive of solidarity—The Christ spirit must prevail.

4   THE SOCIAL MESSAGE OF JESUS

CHAPTER   PAGE

V. The Master's Kingdom Ideals.................. 53
His intimate yet detached viewpoint: the place of
clear vision and hope—Individual soundness at the
basis of social improvement—Personal salvation
needed—The reclamation of social relations through
service—Service a life principle proclaimed and prac-
ticed by Jesus—Orientation with respect to God—
The Master's purpose to do God's will.

VI. A New Dynamic............................... 63
The simple plan of social change—Contrast with
other social plans—An amazing purpose—Transformation of life in two aspects—Christian love an adequate motive power.

VII. Is There Progress?........................... 74
Reasons for thinking that social change is contemplated in the plan of Jesus—The social duties
laid upon His followers—The original aim of the
church—Position of present-day individualists—
Four tests of the essential Christianity of social
institutions.

PART TWO

SOME PRACTICAL APPLICATIONS OF THE GOSPEL'S TEACHING

VIII. The Family................................... 87
An ancient and important institution—Divorce a
world-wide evil—Effect of changed industrial conditions—Socialization of family functions—Entrance
of women into industry—Christ's ideals of the family and marriage: permanence, highly esteemed,
divinely appointed.

IX. The School.................................... 98
Its gradual democratization—Connection between
education and the church—Weakness in religious
education—Peril of the situation—Christian standards in education.

CONTENTS 5

CHAPTER   PAGE

X. THE STATE.................................... 108
Definition and classification—Functions of the state
— War — Legislation — Punishment — Relations of
Christians to the state.

XI. THE SHOP AND THE MART...................... 118
The complexity of industrial life—Child labor,
extent and results—Women and girls in gainful occupations, results and causes—The grim toll of
industrial accidents—Sweat shops—Practical mammonism.

XII. PLAY... 129
Changed attitudes toward recreation and amuse-
ments—Educational value of play—Increased leisure
—Attitude of criminologists—The church and amuse-
ments—The problem of commercialized amusements
—Socialized pageantry—Other activities.

PART THREE

THE CHALLENGE TO THE CHURCH

XIII. A SPIRITUAL BASIS FOR SOCIAL IDEALS............ 143
The value of spiritual ideals; their effect in prevent-
ing a materialistic emphasis—A spiritual basis essential to successful social reform—Contentment needs
a spiritual basis—The spiritual lays hold on power—
The social message does not minimize the personal
gospel.

XIV. THE CHALLENGE TO THE CHURCH.................. 152
Evidenced by the present critical conditions—The
gospel's message of brotherhood a further evidence—
The church is also challenged by a disposition to
ignore it as a social factor—Opposition of some
social leaders—Foreign conceptions of the church—
Responsibility of the church for this estrangement—
Use of criticism—Forces of evil threaten the very
existence of the church—Failure of some Christians
to understand this challenge.

CONTENTS

CHAPTER   PAGE

XV. THE CHANCE OF THE CHURCH.................... 163
    An opportunity for leadership—A fourfold social
    program; instruction about social problems; a study
    of the gospel; direct cooperation; development of
    leaders—The church's greatest task is setting up
    ideals—Its contribution will be to overcome mate-
    rialism.

BIBLIOGRAPHY 172

INTRODUCTION

The nineteenth century discovered the historical Christ. The twentieth century is beginning to take him seriously. Systematic theology has been more interested in the gospel about Jesus than in the gospel which he himself preached. The result has been that the social bearing of Christianity has been, one might almost say, incidental to its interest in post-mortem salvation. Strictly speaking, there is only one gospel, but it has social as well as individual application. There is no necessity of conflict between preparation for life after death and preparation for life in society. Jesus makes no such distinction. It is only misunderstanding which can account for the charge that those who believe that the message of Jesus is applicable to society are belittling the need of the conversion of the individual. On the contrary, some of the most insistent pleas for the development of a Christ-like attitude through faith will be found in volumes concerned with what has loosely been called the social gospel.

It is well to emphasize the fact that the ethics of Jesus rested upon his religion. It is useless to talk about the finality of love if God himself is a blind force or merely a heartless Creator. It is religious faith to which the teaching of Jesus appeals, not only as a basis for ideals, but as the source of power for enduring the self-sacrifice which those ideals involve. Such an attitude is far enough from that of a mere student of society or a mere

7

writer of Utopias. The kingdom of God has to be made up of men who possess love like God's. To get men to grow like God is Jesus' method of making them suitable material for a social order. The principles of the social order grow out of the same conception.

Approach to the social implications and applications of such a fundamental religious attitude lies, on the one side, through a knowledge of the teaching of Jesus and on the other side through a knowledge of economics and sociology. A noble religious purpose must not be used to justify unintelligent social ethic. It is one thing to want to be good and another thing to be wise as well as good.

The present volume illustrates these general considerations. A generation has passed since the first modern writings on the social teaching of Jesus began to appear, but if the present volume lacks the novelty of pioneering, it has the advantage of experience. Unless I quite mistake, it represents in clear and unbiased fashion the general results of modern research in its field. It will serve an admirable purpose if it can help the generation that must remake our world interest itself in the principles of Jesus Christ. The world has tried pretty nearly every means of maintaining the social structure. The tragedies attending every unethical method ought to commend that proposed by Jesus Christ.

SHAILER MATHEWS.

PREFACE

SINCE the pioneer works of Peabody, Mathews, and Rauschenbusch appeared, now nearly a score of years ago, many phases of the relationship of Christianity to social progress have been discussed. The suspicion with which these earlier studies were too often regarded has given way to wide-spread interest. On the whole the church to-day believes in social progress and that true and permanent progress is conditioned on the principles of Jesus' gospel. Christian people are acquiring social vision, and the enlarging circle of problems is regarded as offering wider scope for making practical application of Christian ideals.

With the increasing number of books treating specific questions there has seemed to be room for a manual to furnish an introduction to a study of the gospel and its social message. During the past ten years the writer has led some dozen classes in such a study, going over the field of the present text in whole or in part. The book is developed from the outlines used and the lecture material accumulated in these studies. It has been tested out in syllabus form with university classes and church training school groups.

Frequent quotations from and citations to other works have been used deliberately, for the writer feels that to bring the student into contact with these master writers will be a real service. The purpose is to supply a guide for class discussions. To this end many "Exercises" have been arranged which are intended to stimulate thought and set the members of the class to work. The teacher should use these as the basis of discussions and as introductory to the study of the chapter itself. A tested and valuable plan is to occasionally assign some of these exercises to be answered briefly in writing.

The "Topics for Further Study" are suitable for longer papers or reports, especially by more mature persons such as college students.

It is felt that sufficient range of treatment has been provided so that this book may be used by Sunday-school classes of young people, college classes, teacher-training classes and many other groups of Christian workers.

The writer is indebted to many sources which space will not permit him to mention in detail. His primary inspiration in the whole subject was from the works of Dr. Shailer Mathews, Professor Walter Rauschenbusch, and Professor Francis G. Peabody.

Dr. Emory S. Bogardus and Dr. John G. Hill have read the manuscript and given many helpful suggestions. Their assistance is gratefully acknowledged.

J. H. M.

PART ONE

THE SOCIAL IMPLICATIONS OF THE GOSPEL

"The true light was that which illumines every man by its coming into the world. He was in the world, and the world came into existence through Him, and the world did not recognize Him. He came to the things that were His own, and His own people gave him no welcome. But all who have received Him, to them—that is, to those who trust in His name—He has given the privilege of becoming children of God" (John 1:9-12, Weymouth Version New Testament).

"Jesus came into Galilee, proclaiming God's Good News. 'The time has fully come,' He said, 'and the Kingdom of God is close at hand: repent and believe this Good News'" (Mark 1:14, 15, Weymouth Version New Testament).

It is in the conviction that the Light is for the illumination of the deep shadows of human society that these chapters have been written.

Part One deals with the social idealism of Jesus. After a necessary discussion of the term "Social Question" it considers the value of Jesus' opinion and the fundamental social conceptions of his teaching. His social vision is binocular—it perceives both the individual and society. Personality and social solidarity are coequal in importance. We then seek further and find great life ideals for the social relations of individuals. These are The Approach to Life from Within, The Reclamation of Social Relations Through Service, the Orientation of Life with God, and that Love is the sufficient dynamic. Specific application to problems is left for later consideration. What is sought now is the statement of the social axioms which form the point of departure for Jesus' social message.

CHAPTER I

THE SOCIAL QUESTION

WHAT is the social question? Into what fields will its study lead us? What are its characteristics? What problems are involved? What message may we expect to find in the gospel for the conditions of modern life? These are among the questions which come to mind in undertaking an examination of the social bearing of the words of Jesus as they are recorded in the New Testament. For a short definition perhaps there is none better than that of Professor Peabody. "The social question," he says, "in its most elementary form, is approached when one becomes aware among the problems of conduct that he is not alone, but a person among other persons, a member of the social order, a part of a social whole." Another statement is, "That collection of problems which have arisen under the burden of social maladjustment."

Human relationships mean mutual responsibilities and duties; duties neglected mean burdens for another to bear. The chafing, the sense of injustice, the lack of opportunity, the lowering of the level of living, the dimming of ideals, on the one hand; the greed, the selfishness, the ruthlessness, the lust for power, on the other—these are the elements of the social question. It is not simply a question of poverty, though it is there that the pressure is heaviest. Neither are these problems merely those of commercial life; the church also feels the impact.

There are many characteristics of the present age which might be selected as historically significant. Among these may be mentioned scientific advance, popular government, the printing press, "big" business, popular education, transportation and communication. More truly significant than any of these is the modern interest in the social question. In fact, the others gain in importance because of this interest. The discoveries of science gain their greatest significance when they are applied to modify the conditions of life. The telephone, radium, improved transportation, anæsthetics, poison gas, commercial dye stuffs are but a few of the contributions of science. And of these, as of most scientific discoveries and developments, it may be said that they are important only as they have affected human happiness, comfort, health, and welfare. The same is true of the other things named as historically significant of these present days. Back of all of them is human society.

A modern problem.—It is indeed a modern problem. This is not because ill-treatment is something new in human relations. One has but to remember Egyptian bondage or Jewish slavery to see that the problems of human relationship have always existed. Consider ancient Rome, or England in the Middle Ages, or colonial America, and the same facts are seen. The present manifestations are, however, modern. Factory, labor union, saloon, slum, millionaire, politics, are all words of the present. Widespread interest in the problem is also modern. There have been individuals in every age with a healthy discontent for the social condition about them. There have been many Ruskins. But widespread interest and the determination to find a cure is of to-day.

It is of importance that we understand the nature of the modernity of the social question, otherwise we may be inclined to wonder whether the gospel can have any message for to-day. Jesus never saw a factory nor encountered a labor organizer. If the modern problems are entirely new, then we might reasonably doubt whether his words would have much application to them. If, on the other hand, these troubles are essentially old and only new in their form of manifestation, then a message may be expected from the gospel.

Ҳ **Radical interest shown.**—In the past all attempts at social reform have been largely ameliorative, but another temper is found to-day. The interest is radical in the best sense of the word. It seeks to get to the root of the matter. The question is not so much of mitigating the evils of the existing order as whether the existing order shall be permitted to continue. As one writer puts it, the interest is not in "social therapeutics but in social bacteriology and hygiene." For example, we are less interested in finding the best methods of doing charitable work than in discovering the reason why poverty exists. Examination is being made of the pillars of the present order, and the question is being asked whether it is worth while to try to mend them and prop them up.

Modern civilization rests on three great institutions, that is, the family, private property, and the state. Each of these is being critically examined to-day and its right to existence challenged. There are those who confidently predict the abolition of each of these, and their arguments are interesting even if not convincing. The significant thing, however, is not so much what these ideas are as that there are such ideas. The important point is that there are those who are willing to entirely abandon the existing social order, to reconstruct it along entirely new lines, to give up institutions which are centuries old—to do anything, in fact, that promises a higher type of life and wider opportunities for mankind. All this is viewed with the utmost alarm by many people. To them it just means discontent and dissatisfaction and disaster. Such people are advocates of the doctrine of *laissez faire*. They are the stand-patters. Their motto is, "Let well enough alone." Their conservative natures are averse to change, and all this talk of uprooting things fills them with terror. Another group see in these plans the dawn of hope; at last the shackles are being broken. Usefulness, not age, is their standard of value. Now, whichever way our mental processes lead us, whether we are conservative or of those who easily welcome change, this much must certainly be clear: the interest in the modern social question is real and deep; it is radical in its nature.

There is hope in this, for when things are wrong discontent is the best possible thing. The sick man who has no symptoms, feels no discomfort, is in a desperate state. Mistakes will be made, of course. The attempt will be made to abandon some things which should be mended, and to hold on to some things which we could well afford to let go. There will be mistakes of the head as well as of the heart. Some men under the sheep's wool of an assumed interest in the social welfare, will try to hide the wolf of selfish purposes. However, out of all this interest we may hope for real progress. One reason for this optimistic view is found in the third characteristic of the social question, namely, that it is essentially a moral question.

Every problem moral at its base.—It is worth careful note that the interest in these problems does not arise out of the bad conditions themselves. There is no "social question" on the Congo or in the heart of China. As Professor Peabody puts it, "The problem of social justice does not grow out of the worst social conditions, but the best. It is not a sign of social decadence but of social vitality." The social problem, as such, emerges when contrasts are drawn between good and bad conditions and when the moral values of the issues are discerned. In fact, no vital question of human welfare is purely economic. A moral issue is always involved, and no such question is finally settled until there is recognition of this moral issue as such. For example, the decision in the Civil War went to the North because it had more men, more money, and more munitions. But the reason that slavery is no longer an issue is not found in that victory; it is, rather, to be found in a nation-wide conviction that slavery is wrong.

The usual arguments offered in favor of the liquor traffic are economic—so many dollars invested, so much paid in wages, so much of tax income for the state. These arguments are often properly met by other statements of economic waste, setting forth the cost of crime and poverty. But in the end this question will not be finally settled until there is a powerful conviction on the part of most people that the thing is wrong, not only economically but morally.

Again, the labor question is not essentially a matter of dollars, of wages on the one hand, or of dividends on the other. It is a matter of justice and the proper treatment of a brother man. Purely economic as industrial disputes may seem to be in many aspects, the crucial point is really always moral. The possible rent and return on the investment are not the sole considerations in building an apartment house. The conditions of life, sanitation, light, safety, comfort—these are at least equally important. The landlord who fails to recognize this and who acquires profit at the expense of his fellow beings is unsocial and unchristian in these relations.

So in whatever direction we turn, whatever problems we consider, we find that the issues are not purely economic, but social and moral as well. In this fact is found the hope of final victory. It also points the way to the gospel as a source of help. Surely, in the solution of these fundamentally moral questions it will not do to neglect the words of the Great Teacher of Morals.

The far reach of the social question.—The social question is, then, as broad as human interest, and is manifested wherever failure in mutual relations has resulted in undue and undeserved burdens. It extends to all the institutions of civilization. The home, the church, education, business, and pleasure alike make their contributions to the group of problems comprehended under this statement. No man is so rich, so poor, so wise or so ignorant as to be outside the circle.

We see that there are three outstanding characteristics of the social question: its modernness, its radical nature, and its moral quality. These must each be kept in mind if we are to give a full account of the matter. As noted above, there is nothing new or modern about the bald facts of human inability to get along well together. It is an outcropping of "natural religion" as old as Cain and Abel. The same spirit of envy that sent Naboth to his death still operates to-day. The manifestations are new. The deep-seated, precedent-destroying radical interest is of to-day. The clearly defined moral issues are more insistently set forth than ever before.

This is the social question with which the gospel of Jesus deals—not in detail, but in general terms. We shall find there no program of welfare work; no discussion of specific problems for the most part. We shall search in vain for exact terms of agreement between capital and labor. What we shall find will be statements of fundamental truth so simply given that their very simplicity has caused them to be neglected. The Golden Rule has seemed so elemental that men have passed it by in search of some profound and intricate guide to agreement.

Our business and that of the church, as will appear in a later chapter, is this: To master on the one hand the spirit and purport of Jesus' teaching, and, on the other, to become familiar with the life conditions of the great human family. From this basis we may proceed with some confidence to apply the teachings to the conditions.

EXERCISES

1. Name five problems which have arisen from "social maladjustment."
2. What is the most common "unsocial" act?
3. Give some reasons for feeling that interest in social welfare is increasing.
4. Have any "new" social abuses developed under modern industry?
5. What is meant by "the interest is not in social therapeutics but in social bacteriology and hygiene"?
6. Consider the foundations of society:
    (a) What are the essential institutions of modern civilization?
    (b) Is it probable that any of these will soon be abolished?
7. Is labor agitation valuable?
8. Is age a sign of value in a social institution?
9. Is it best to be conservative or progressive?
10. Compare the social situations of the following: A working man of the first century and of to-day; a citizen of New York and of Shanghai; a farm hand in Kansas and a mechanic in the Ford automobile factory.
11. Where would you expect to find the worst social conditions? where the best? In which place could improvement be most easily secured?
12. Is it true that no question is purely economic?
13. Can you cite a social issue involving no moral considerations?

14. Has the Bible anything to say about industrial accidents? Does it give any valuable principles for dealing with their prevention?

TOPICS FOR FURTHER STUDY

1. Compare the lot of a workingman in the first century with that of one in America to-day.
2. The slums of Jerusalem.
3. Has the family outlived its usefulness?
4. Social movements outside of Christian influence.
5. The modern social problem and the industrial revolution.

SUGGESTED READINGS

Batten, *The Social Task of Christianity*, pp. 33–37.
Peabody, *Jesus Christ and the Social Question*, pp. 1–12.
Whitaker, *The Gospel at Work in Modern Life*, Chapter I.

CHAPTER II

THE MASTER'S APPRAISAL OF LIFE

In the suburbs of a beach city in California there lived a man who knew a great deal about seashells. Not long ago there was held in this same city a meeting of a society of conchologists, but for some reason this man refused to go. The society, however, took a recess and went to seek him.

There is no man in the world whose opinion about electric storage batteries is more valuable than that of Thomas A. Edison. Half a dozen years or so ago he gave a newspaper interview on the subject of immortality. Tests made of various audiences by the writer indicate that not ten people in a hundred remember having seen this interview in print, and not one in a hundred can tell what he said.

We find on the program of a high-school commencement an oration on the "Modern Trend of Industrialism," and we smile.

A witness gives his testimony in court and is then subjected to a grilling cross examination, through which the opposing counsel hopes to develop some contradiction or mistake.

A writer charges a "leak" in Wall Street, writes of manipulations, and fills many pages of a popular magazine with tales of "frenzied finance." People adopt the term, forget the author, except to wonder what he got out of it, and refuse to get excited.

Speaking with authority.—What is an authority? Whose opinions do we value? To insure the authoritative note there must at least be these qualities: First, detailed knowledge to give familiarity with the object at hand. This is why the California conchologist was sought out by his fellow scientists. It also explains why Edison's words carry great weight in one field and but little in another. Then there must be general knowledge gained through experience to furnish background and insure good judgment. The high-school graduate may put facts together in a logical fashion, but we fail to be impressed, for we are not sure of his sound judgment. He has no background of life experience. The third essential is accuracy. If the testimony of a witness is shaken even in minor matters, the whole is discredited. Then, lastly, there must be disinterestedness. We do not trust the man "with an ax to grind," for it is hard for him to be fair even if he is honest.

With these ideas in mind, let us consider the Master's appraisal of life and ask if it has value. It is recorded of him that when he discoursed of prayer and false teachers and obedience the crowds were filled with amazement at his teaching, "for he had been teaching them as *one* having authority, and not as their scribes" taught.[1] When he brings his report and impressions of life and speaks concerning the social relations of men, will it carry to us that same note of authority?

Jesus knew and understood life.—Notice, first of all, that he experienced life. In three short years he lived more than some folks do in ten times as

---

[1] Matthew 7: 29.

long. So many people live in a limited circle. Day after day and year after year they talk to the same sort of people, attend the same sort of meetings, hear the same sort of preaching, read the same sort of books and papers, vote for the same sort of politicians, wear the same sort of clothes, eat the same sort of food, and think the same sort of thoughts. Moving from city to city may change the surroundings, but the essential routine of life is the same. It almost seems that nothing short of a world war can jar them into new orbits. Jesus, on the other hand, lived intensely and with a wide range of experience. He met all sorts of people. Levi, the tax-gatherer; Jairus, a president of the synagogue; Mary, Martha, and Lazarus, well-to-do citizens of Bethany; Nicodemus, a ruler of the Jews; Herod, king of Judæa; the group of fishermen, his disciples; Luke, the physician; blind beggars and wretched lepers by the wayside; Pharisees and scribes; Roman soldiers and officers.

This list but suggests the variety which marked his acquaintance with people. Then look at the places where he is found. On the streets, in the Temple, at various homes, by the country roadside, at the market, in the fields, by the side of lake and river, at feasts and weddings and funerals and banquets. It is to be remembered, too, that these are but the comparatively few incidents recorded in the Gospels and that, as John tells us, "there are also many other things which Jesus did" —so vast a number, indeed, that if they were all described in detail, "I suppose that even the world itself would not contain the books that should be written."[2]

_____
[2] John 21: 25.

The point, however, lies not so much in the variety of people he met; the average American child of twelve years possibly has had more opportunities for social contacts. It is, rather, in the thoroughness of the contacts, in the use he made of them. He used to the utmost his opportunities of learning life. No incident was too trivial to make its contribution to his store of knowledge about human beings. We can feel some of this because of his instant and understanding sympathy with all sorts of people in all kinds of circumstances. Such breadth and depths of appreciation of human needs does not come from a shallow or limited contact with life.

Again we find that Jesus' observation of life is penetrating, and his report of facts and estimate of character are accurate. In this connection read again these incidents. The discussion about unwashed hands, in Matthew 15: 1–20, represents the scribes and Pharisees coming to him with a criticism of the disciples for their neglect of a ceremonial custom. His reply, pointing out their own shortcomings, was much more than just a turning of their question back upon themselves. The disciples were deficient in mere legal formality, but the fault of the scribes lay deeper, as Jesus so keenly observed. Again, in Matthew 7: 16 he reasons clearly about judgment, while in Matthew 23: 1–33 is another incisive estimate of the "blind leaders of the blind." It was pretty hard for a Jew to see any good in one of his countrymen who grew wealthy collecting taxes for Rome, but Jesus quickly estimated Zacchæus as a man worth a visit (Luke 19: 1–10). The Sadducees came to him with one of their endless questions about the resurrection (Matthew 22: 23–33). His reply, although ignoring the specific question, drove to the very heart of the whole matter and laid bare their ignorance of their own Scriptures. Again Jesus displayed a keen insight into their purpose.

Consider just one other of the many examples of the accuracy and penetrating power found in Jesus' estimate of character. In John 3: 1–21 is found the account of the profound discussion with Nicodemus. This learned man comes to him with no carping, futile questions such as the others, considered already, had propounded. Jesus meets him on his own level and answers him fully and profoundly. It is illuminating when we think of the mind of the Master to note how he quickly detected insincerity and met it with stinging reproof, but just as quickly rewarded real interest with an answer exactly suited to the questioner's mental ability.

From these incidents and many others like them we learn another thing about the Master's estimate of life: it is a great thing to observe correctly; it is even greater to be able to think correctly about the things observed. To do this requires good judgment. Jesus' power in this direction is evidenced by his wise replies.

Notice next that Jesus' view of life was unbiased and comprehensive. The usual engrossing personal details of living had little hold upon him. His reply to the would-be follower by the lakeside was doubtless primarily for the purpose of testing his sincerity, but it also puts into a vivid phrase this same fact: "Foxes have holes and birds have nests, but the Son of Man has nowhere to lay His head." The glimpses of his family life which we have indicate that these relations were ideal; but nevertheless these family ties were transcended by his interest in humanity. (Matthew 12: 46–50.) Our views of life's problems are colored by our own needs and circumstances. It is almost impossible, for example, to think clearly and correctly about the evident power of wealth, whether our bias be that of poverty or possession. We are constantly exposed to the warping influence of self-interest. Jesus was free from such trammels. He was of life, knew it intimately, felt its touch, and understood its cries of distress; but at the same time he was free from the entanglements of life and from its cramping, distorting, dwarfing influences. Not that he never felt their pull, but, rather, that he resisted and conquered them.

Finally, his view of life is authoritative and divine. Human views of life are at best but partial guesses. His bears the stamp of authority. "My teaching does not belong to me, but comes from Him who sent me,"[3] he says. Again, in the high-priestly prayer, he exclaims, "The truths which thou didst teach me I have taught them. And they have received them and have known for certain that I came out from thy presence, and have believed that thou didst send me."[4]

"In his teaching, Jesus rested upon his own authority as absolute. He did not hesitate to place

---

[3] John 7: 16, Weymouth Version New Testament. Used by permission of Congregational Publication Society, American distributors.

[4] John 17: 6–8. Weymouth Version New Testament.

his own word above the Mosaic law; he proclaimed his message now as his own, now as his heavenly Father's, with no distinction; he taught his disciples to look to him as their only means of entrance into the higher life (John 14: 16)—a colossal assumption surely, if he were but a man; a clear statement and a challenge to all the ages, sublime in its boldness, but justified by the divine greatness of his character, the matchless sublimity of his teaching, and proved to succeeding generations by the historic success of his work."[5]

The Master's appraisal of life has value.—It is worth while then to know the Master's appraisal of life. He lived intensely, touching life at many points and thereby gaining an intimate and comprehensive knowledge of human kind. From this knowledge he reports accurately, thus establishing one of the first essentials of an authoritative statement. Next we found keenness of insight and soundness of judgment as revealed by every reported conversation. These are also to be added to the evidence for the value of his decisions. Again, his judgments are free from self-interest, that great warper of men's judgment. His intense interest in life was never complicated by his personal problems. It is worth while, too, to know that the perfect unity with the Father expressed in the words, "I and my Father are one," insures that when we know the thought and plan of Jesus we glimpse the thought and plan of God.

One might acquire great technical skill as a musician and be ignorant of Beethoven or Liszt,

[5]Jenks' *Social Significance of the Teachings of Jesus*, p. 39. Association Press, New York.

but the earnest student knows the work of the masters. The field of literature is rich and varied, and wide excursions might be made which omitted familiarity with Shakespeare, but it would be a strange culture which neglected the Bard of Avon. It is possible to go far in science alone or by following the lesser lights, but the wise seeker after nature's secrets sits at the feet of Newton, Agassiz, and Pasteur. When we study mankind, then, can we dare to neglect the One who in a few words spoken during a few brief years transformed human living?

Often on a winter evening, when a freezing rain has fallen, the ice-covered twigs and branches seem to form a glittering maze. Then turning toward some bright light the reflections are such that a series of concentric circles are seen about that light. History is a mass of confused, apparently unrelated events. Human life is a perplexity, a tangle. Good men work at cross purposes. There seems to be neither law nor order anywhere. All is a tangle, hopeless and discouraging. Then if we can but fix our eyes on Jesus Christ all these twisted bits of human existence fall into ordered relationship to each other and to him, their center and pivot.

"Show me Thy face—I shall forget
    The weary days of yore,
The fretting ghosts of vain regret
    Shall haunt my soul no more.
All doubts and fears for future years
    In quiet trust subside,
And naught but blest content and calm
    Within my heart abide."

(Anonymous.)

1. Why is the judgment of a person who is slow to express an opinion usually valued more highly than that of a talkative person?
2. Name an authority in music; government; business. What constitutes the basis of authority in each case?
3. Should the head of a business concern himself with the small details of his organization?
4. Is breadth of an acquaintance essential to understanding life? Does it insure such understanding?
5. Give an original example of the warping effect upon judgment of self-interest.
6. Would the professional opinion of a physician seem less valuable to you if you knew that he had low moral standards? of a musician? of a politician?
7. Of two persons, one with broad experience and education and the other with a limited outlook, which will probably form the most fixed and absolute estimate of another person? Which will form the most accurate estimate?
8. Give an original reason for thinking that Jesus' estimate of life is valuable.
9. Cite incidents from Jesus' life showing
    (a) His broad acquaintance with life.
    (b) His insight into character.
    (c) His clear estimate of character.
    (d) His freedom from personal bias.
    (e) The authoritative note in his statements.
10. Did the religious insight of Jesus reenforce or diminish his social feeling?

TOPICS FOR FURTHER STUDY

1. The types of character found among the acquaintances of Jesus.
2. Were Jesus' power of penetration and keenness of judgment superhuman?
3. The place of the detached view in social service.
4. The divine plan for human life as revealed in Jesus' teaching and example.
5. The source of authority in Jesus' teaching.

SUGGESTED READINGS

Jenks, *Social Significance of the Teachings of Jesus*, Study II.

Rauschenbusch, *Christianizing the Social Order*, pp. 40–47.

Peabody, *Jesus Christ and the Social Question*, Chapter 1.

CHAPTER III

THE WORTH OF A MAN

THE solution of the social question may be approached in two radically differing ways. One concerns itself primarily with the individual and chooses its methods accordingly. Consideration is given to his happiness, his rights, his needs, his duties, and his development in character. Society and social institutions are considered to exist only that they may serve the individual and when they cease so to function are felt to have outlived their usefulness. A school, for example, may be an object of civic pride, its buildings an ornament to the neighborhood, and its teachers accomplished members of the community. There is, however, no real reason for its existence unless boys and girls are gathered under its roof and benefited by its instruction. Where there is an entirely adult population it would be manifestly absurd to maintain a kindergarten. Such a condition does actually exist for a time in a frontier town or a mining camp. Under this theory, when readjustments of social relations become necessary, they must commence with the individual.

For example, consider the vexed problem of capital and labor. This method would ask such questions as: What is a fair day's work? How much is a proper wage? What is a sufficient profit on investment? It would seek, in other words, to have both employer and employee occupy a right attitude toward the rights, necessities, and duties of the other, confident that they can work out with justice to both in all the details of the situation.

The other view takes society collectively as the object of interest and constructive effort. The individual recedes into the background; becomes just one of the mass, a social unit. Reforms are to be accomplished "en masse." Of course, ultimately individuals will be benefited, but that often seems almost a secondary matter. The process proposed, at least, is something like this: Get social institutions right, make the adjustments, correct the errors of organization, and then the rights of the individual will be conserved and his happiness and comfort assured.

Using again the relation of capital and labor as an example, this method of seeking a solution would endeavor to change the system and establish new methods of cooperation in work. It recognizes, of course, the need of a changed attitude on the part of individuals, but would bring that about by changing the outer conditions of life.

Any complete program of social progress must include both of these methods to some extent. As will be seen later, in considering some of the proposed social philosophies, a plan which ignores the dynamic of changed individual lives is doomed to failure. Just as truly this dynamic cannot be limited to the small circle of personal interests; it must be brought to bear upon the tasks of common welfare.

Jesus' approach to the social question.—Of these two methods of approach the former is the one which Jesus employs. "Jesus did not work for the Jewish nation or the Roman Empire or society as a whole. He worked first of all for souls—sinful men and women. The first great message of the social gospel is just this: men and women can be saved from sin each by himself or herself. Nobody has to wait for good legislation or good sewerage or good customs or good food or good times or a good world. Only think where the prodigal son began, where the woman who anointed Jesus at the house of Simon began. If either had waited till society had been regenerated, they might be waiting to-day. . . .

"There has been no little discussion as to whether the individual or society is the great end of all social development. From the Christian point of view there need be no hesitancy in the answer so far as man is concerned: the saved individual is the supreme end of the divine will. Only it is the *saved* individual; that is, one whose life is like God's as it appears in Jesus. And that, of course, means not a selfish, narrow, egotistic individualism, but one that is social, full of love and helpfulness—a life that finds its proper expression only in the community of other lives like itself. In other words, there can be no real regenerate life that is anti-social. To use the dialect of the schools, the saved life must function socially or be lost."[1]

A high estimate of personality.—Jesus had a high appreciation of the worth of a man. He was always ready to stop and talk to individuals. Each

[1] Mathews, *The Social Gospel*, pp. 12-13 and 14-15.

such conversation he regarded as an opportunity, a chance to state again the simple but comprehensive ideas of the Kingdom. Many such conversations are recorded in the Gospels, while the sermons are but few. Some of his choicest truths were given in conversation with single individuals. The "little gospel" which has been the text of multitudes of sermons came at the conclusion of that memorable talk with Nicodemus. The clear statement about true worship being of the heart was addressed to the woman by the well in Samaria, while it was to Martha that Jesus spoke those words which have brought comfort to so many sorrowing hearts, "I am the resurrection and the life." It is not the present worth of the individual, however, that is Jesus' main concern. It is the future possibilities that he has also, perhaps chiefly, in mind. Folk are precious to him because they may become children of God and joint heirs with Christ. He is aware of their potential worth as members of the Kingdom and concerned that full development shall take place.

This same idea of the worth of the individual is prominent in the teaching of the parables. The gaining of one individual for the Kingdom was the cause of rejoicing in heaven. One lost sheep was sufficient reason for an all-night search by the shepherd.[2] The woman who lost one of her coins sweeps and searches until she finds it, and again there is great joy. The whole parable of the prodigal son, speaking eloquently of the father's love and so figuring the love of God for men, is centered on the one son. These parables also give

[2] Luke 15: 1–10.

us the reason for this high valuation which the Master places upon the worth of a man. To Jesus men and women are of supreme value, not because of what they are, but because of what they may become. It is this chance to become children of God which makes the Christian estimate of men so high.

Consider also that his teachings are individualistic; they are about duties for a man, not for men. It is possible for one to be a follower of Christ all by oneself, even among those who are hostile and out of sympathy. Men can be saved all by themselves. The drunkard may reform and need not wait for the saloon to be abolished. This is seen also in his teaching that worship is an individual matter. The Hebrew thought of worship as dependent on place and priest and ritual, but Jesus pointed out that not place but the spirit of worship was the essential thing.[3]

This lesson has not been thoroughly learned even after nineteen centuries. Out of four hundred and forty-seven millions of nominal Christians in the world, three hundred and twenty-eight millions, or nearly seventy per cent, adhere to a form of worship depending on a ritual conducted in a language which they do not understand. Furthermore, many a Protestant service is at its best a time to hear a sermon and receive instruction or inspiration, and at its lowest a performance by minister and choir to be enjoyed (weak word of small minds) and criticized. Without forgetting in the least the helpfulness of a beautiful service or an eloquent sermon, still what a need there is for Christians to "worship in spirit and in truth"!

---
[3] John 4: 19–24.

So it is with other matters. Jesus has the highest regard for personality. In that dramatic scene where the woman taken in adultery is brought before him he senses what her accusers have missed —that her personality has been debased and degraded, but that there still remains a spark of humanity. It was his high regard for human worth, even when brought low through sin, that enabled him to handle a difficult situation with consummate tact. As Dr. Rauschenbush says: "This regard for human life was based on the same social instinct which every normal man possesses. But with Jesus it was so strong that it determined all his viewpoints and activities. He affirmed the humane instinct consciously and intelligently and raised it to the dignity of a social principle."

The most convincing proof, however, of the estimate which Jesus placed on the worth of a man is that he committed the interests of his kingdom to the care of a few individuals. When a great movement is launched in these days, what complicated machinery is deemed needful! There must be a constitution and by-laws and officers and committees and resolutions. A propaganda must be worked out and a policy determined on. Mass meetings must be called, intensive campaigns launched, speeches made, and books written. An official organ must be started and an endowment raised. Then, when results are counted up, the whole "movement" sometimes is ludicrously like using a steam sawmill, with its flying belts and ponderous machines, to sharpen a lead pencil. Men plan and contrive and strain and fail. Jesus speaks a few simple truths, plants a dynamic force in the hearts of a few followers, and his work endures for centuries, transforming the generations. It was indeed the placing of a very little leaven in a very great lump, but the results justify the wisdom of the means.

In the beginning God created man in his own image. It is the profound realization of this truth that determines the estimate which the Master places on the worth of a man. None are so humble or unworthy as to be beneath his attention. The image of his Father may be sadly defaced, but it may be restored. The possibilities of development are so infinitely great that Jesus says to his disciples, "Be ye also perfect, even as your Father which is in heaven is perfect." When Jesus' recognition of the dignity and worth of men and women becomes the universal standard, then social reconstruction will soon be an accomplished fact.

The hall mark of Christianity.—This realization of "the worth of a man" has been one of the hall marks of Christianity. Other great faiths of mankind have contributed to religious truth, but they have uniformly fallen short at this point. When Christianity penetrates heathendom and supplants its civilization, charitable aid, hospitals, orphanages, and similar institutions quickly follow. Human life is safer and living more worth while under the shadow of the cross. Womanhood is put upon a new level. An Arab proverb says, "The threshold weeps forty days when a girl is born." A common Chinese saying declares, "If a girl does no harm, it is enough; you cannot expect her to be either useful or good." Contrast these statements and the attitude toward woman which they typify with the place of woman in Christian lands. In the same way childhood is honored and the potentialities of individuality recognized again.

But if "the worth of a man" supplies a test when two civilizations are put in contrast, it is also available in determining the genuineness of the Christianity of so-called Christian institutions. If we find that "Business as now constituted, has a constitutional and inevitable interest in raising the value of Things and keeping down the value of Men," or that "Whenever Life is set above Profit in business there is a thrill of admiration which indicates that something unusual has been done," we are certainly entitled to at least suspect a difference between the ideals of business and the ideals of Christ. It is safe to say that whatever degrades man is displeasing to God. The stout warnings of Amos were directed toward those "which oppress the poor, which crush the needy" and "that lie upon beds of ivory, and stretch themselves upon their couches, . . . but they are not grieved for the affliction of Joseph." That word is not out of date. Oppression, though form and occasion may change, is as eternally wrong in America to-day as in Israel long centuries ago.

"The principle of reverence for personality is the ruling principle in ethics and in religion; it constitutes, therefore, the truest and highest test of either an individual or a civilization; it has been, even unconsciously, the guiding and determining principle in all human progress; and in its religious interpretation it is, indeed, the one faith that keeps meaning and value for life" (President Henry C. King).

1. By what standards do we usually value men?
2. Give an illustration of the fact that the advancement of a civilization may be judged by the estimate placed on individuals.
3. Is there a relation between community morals and child-labor statistics?
4. Is it true that "Prostitution is the worst form of contempt for personality"?
5. Give some evidences that modern society values men apart from their economic utility.
6. Give examples of modern legislation based on a keen appreciation of "the worth of a man."
7. Show that race prejudice discounts the worth of the individual.
8. When does "personal liberty" become "license"?
9. May the community restrict "personal liberty" through legislation without violating personality?
10. Give reasons for believing that Jesus values individuals highly.
11. Why do you think it was that Jesus depended on individual action rather than on organization for the promotion of his cause?
12. Was the valuation placed by Jesus on the individual ahead of that common at that time?
13. Which should come first, individual reform or legislation? Apply this to prohibition of the use of intoxicants.
14. Is it true that a man cannot be saved all by himself?

TOPICS FOR FURTHER STUDY

1. The church is made for man, not man for the church.
2. The conversations of Jesus.
3. The social value of worship.
4. The primacy of the individual in social work.
5. Restoring the image of God.

SUGGESTED READINGS

Mathews, *The Social Gospel*, Chapter I.

Batten, *The Social Task of Christianity*, pp. 74–83.

Jenks, *Social Significance of the Teachings of Jesus*, Study IV.

Rauschenbusch, *The Social Principles of Jesus*, Chapter I.

CHAPTER IV

BROTHERHOOD

FELLOWSHIP is vital. Man is a social being and
can by no means reach his best development alone.
It seems almost paradoxical, but it is nevertheless
true that the individual makes his normal and
finest growth when in close contact with others.
Joy, pleasure, service, goodness itself are social in
their nature. The most fearful punishment is
solitary confinement, and the hermit is promptly
recognized as abnormal and almost unhuman. This
fellowship has many manifestations. Cooperative
labor, the team work of the athletic contest, the
worshiping congregation, the family circle, the labor
union, all give their testimony to the fundamental
sociality of human kind. Even "the slender thread
of good in the saloon is comradeship."

Solidarity supreme.—Jesus not only had a high
opinion of the worth of the individual, but he also
stressed the relations between individuals. He
believed in the solidarity of the human family.
As has already been indicated, the salvation of the
individual is truly the object of the Master's interest.
But that very salvation has social results. In fact,
it is true in a certain sense that one cannot "be
saved" by himself. The changed heart of the
individual must give evidence of that change through
its social actions. James gave a correct statement
of the relation of these two parts of Christian expe-

rience when he wrote, "What good is it, my brethren, if a man profess to have faith, and yet his actions do not correspond? Can such faith save him? Suppose a Christian brother or sister is poorly clad or lacks daily food, and one of you says to them, 'I wish you well, keep yourselves warm and well fed,' and yet you do not give them what they need; what is the use of that? So also faith, if it is unaccompanied by obedience, has no life in it—so long as it stands alone." He then refers to Abraham and his willingness to obey, even to the point of sacrificing his son Isaac, and adds, "You see that it is because of actions that a man is pronounced righteous, and not simply because of faith."[1]

It is here that the social implications of the gospel message appear. Jesus begins with the individual, but moves at once to his social relationships. The truth of this is apparent from at least four considerations. Think first of the answer that Jesus gave when asked the question, "Which is the greatest commandment?" It was, of course, in the minds of his questioners a mere quibble about the multitudinous requirements of the Jewish ritual. Jesus, in his reply, points out one central, controlling law—the law of love; and two objects for its exercise—God and brother man.[2] This is fundamental. As Dr. Rauschenbusch points out, "Whoever demands love demands solidarity. Whoever sets love first sets fellowship high."[3] It is on such a foundation of mutual love that the unity of the home rests. Common interests and common fears,

---

[1] James 2: 14-16, 24, Weymouth Version New Testament.
[2] Matthew 22: 35-40.
[3] *The Social Principles of Jesus*, p. 17. Association Press.

cooperation in labor and the sharing of danger are cohesive forces tending to unify the groups on which they operate, but none of them can compare with love. And since it is in the home above all other social institutions that love reigns, it is there that the greatest social unity is found. Later on we shall need to define this form of love and examine its operation. Just now let us be content to regard it as the force which binds the human race into one brotherhood.

A second evidence of Jesus' regard for human solidarity is found in the lengths to which he would go to avoid its violation. Peter came to him with the question, "How oft shall my brother sin against me and I forgive him? Until seven times?" Perhaps Peter felt a glow of self-commendation in setting the limit so high. The rabbinic rule of three times would have put quite a strain on his impetuous nature, but he was willing to go even to the "perfect" number of seven. His legalistic training was shown in the desire to have a definite rule. How amazed he must have been at the Master's "seventy times seven," setting forth the principle of a practically unlimited exercise of the forgiving spirit. This has been called "Christ's most striking innovation in morality." In the succeeding parable of the unforgiving servant,[4] this idea is developed and stated as one of the characteristics of the kingdom of heaven. In this connection consider also the teaching about revenge, in Matthew 5: 38–42; about murder, in Matthew 5: 21–22; about reconciliation, in Matthew 5: 23–26; and the final separation of the sheep and the goats in Matthew 25: 31–46.

[4] Matthew 18: 23–35.

Note that in all these cases fellowship has been
destroyed and that the spirit of Christianity demands an attempt to restore fellowship. Indeed,
so important did this seem to Jesus that he puts
the maintenance of fellowship above "personal
rights." To "turn the other cheek" has become a
misinterpreted byword of spiritless submission.
The whole passage in which it occurs is really an
exaltation of fellowship. It is well to keep in mind
that this has to do with the resenting of personal
injuries, and that no warrant is given for a theory
of nonresistance to the evil influences which are
threatening to disrupt fellowship. Personality is
sacred and must not be transgressed, but it may
forfeit that right by its own unsocial actions. Jesus
himself did not hesitate to condemn when occasion
demanded, and to resist those whose opposition
threatened the success of his work. Read again
his indignant, scornful words against the Pharisees
(Matthew 23: 23–28), and the parable of Dives
(Luke 16: 19–23), and the account of his resistance
to personal temptation (Matthew 4: 8–11; Mark
8: 31–33).

Again Jesus gave evidence of his firm faith in the
solidarity of the race by identifying himself with it.
The term which he frequently applied to himself
was "Son of man." It is not strange that the
beloved John should be the one to record that
expression of affection where the Master says, "I
have called you friends" (John 15: 15). That
friendly spirit of his was exercised in so catholic a
fashion that his critics were moved to sneeringly
say that he ate and fraternized with sinners. But
this attitude of friendliness, this identification of

himself with the great human family, was not shown alone in proffers of helpfulness. Jesus not only contributed but he demanded friendship, which is always a reciprocal relation. Consider in this connection the scene in the garden of Gethsemane.

Finally, it is God's purpose that men should be bound together in unity. This can be indicated by many words from the gospel, but the spirit of them all is gathered into one expression in the First Epistle of John (4: 7-8), "Beloved, let us love one another; for love is of God; and everyone that loveth is born of God, and knoweth God. He that loveth not knoweth not God; for God is love."

The implications of solidarity.—There are some important implications growing out of this fact of the solidarity of the race. One of these is the social conscience and responsibility of the group. A town or neighborhood, or a college class or a church or nation, is more than a collection of persons. Such a social group is an organism, not simply an organization. Jesus recognizes this ' responsibility in the case of Chorazin, Bethsaida, and Capernaum (Matthew 11: 20-24). "We know that by constant common action a social group develops a common spirit and common standards of action, which then assimilate and standardize the actions of its members. Jesus felt the solidarity of the neighborhood groups in Galilee with whom he mingled. He treated them as composite personalities, jointly responsible for their moral decisions."[5]

Group consciousness and group conscience do not always develop together. It is rather easy to incite

[5] Rauschenbusch, *The Social Principles of Jesus*, p. 21.

a crowd of college freshmen to such a consciousness of college traditions and class action that they
will sweep the bleachers, wear green caps, and
collect material for the annual bonfire. To get them
to accept responsibility for the looting of a neighboring lumber yard in the interest of that bonfire
is not so simple. Civic pride in population, new
manufactories, and public buildings is usually
strong. To get the same people to face the revelation of a thorough social survey is another story.
Denominational pride does not always mean denominational progress. Nevertheless, the responsibility
of the social group is an unavoidable fact. The
more completely this responsibility is accepted the
more nearly does any community deserve the term
"Christian."

We must realize this fact of solidarity, for it is
fundamental. We may not like people, but we
cannot be indifferent to them. As Carlyle says,
"In vain thou deniest it, thou art my brother."
It is important to understand just what is meant
by social unity. Modern life is complex and our
needs and interests are inextricably interwoven.
You get up in the morning and turn on the faucet,
confident that the water with which to wash your
face will promptly flow. The gas you cook by,
the light overhead, and the milk on the back steps
are all part of the practically unfailing routine of
your life. Let one of them fail and you feel, and
rightly enough, a sense of ill treatment. When
there is no failure it is because the engineers in the
pumping station, the firemen in the gas works, the
electricians in the power house, and the milkman
on his early morning rounds have done their part

in the world's work. Your comfort and well-being depend on their social faithfulness. In return you have your duties and play your part. These and scores of other such relations involving our physical well-being are easily understood.

Neither must it be forgotten that in many less obvious ways we are interrelated. The store of knowledge which we each possess is made up of many contributions from others. If it were possible to live an absolutely isolated life, it would be devoid of interest. Robinson Crusoe was cut off from physical communication with his fellows for a season, but his mental connections were still maintained. You cannot imagine such a story written about a castaway with no previous experience to draw upon. It is interesting, if somewhat humbling, to see how largely our stock of ideas is borrowed. We lay tribute on teachers, friends, preachers, books, papers, and draw but little from original sources. What do we know of history or science or any other chosen field, except what we have read or been told? The best claim that most of us can make to originality is in rearranging the ideas and drawing a few conclusions. The more we consider, the more we see our interdependence in the mental world.

Again, in the moral realm we are tied to others with a web of invisible but restraining bonds. The balance is so delicate that the defection of one in even some seemingly entirely personal matter disturbs the whole economy. A sulky child in the family casts a cloud on the whole group. It is true that if "one member suffers, all the members suffer." But, happily, the reverse is also true, and righteousness and the uplifting emotions are also contagious. In no way is the essential solidarity of mankind so convincingly evidenced as when the helpful life of some individual brings hope and cheer to a great circle of those even outside his immediate acquaintance. The whole world is lifted by the fervor of a Wesley, or the missionary zeal of a Carey. Sunshine was shed by Florence Nightingale on more hospital cots than she ever visited. In fighting the "Battle with the Slum" Jacob Riis won victories in other dark places than those of New York.

When considering the various problems of social life it is scarcely possible to overestimate the significance of human solidarity. Progress is made when cooperation replaces individual effort or competition. If employer and employee approach their mutual perplexities in the spirit of brotherhood, how much more possible does a just and satisfactory settlement become! Their interests—physical, social, and spiritual—are so intertwined that the only permanent basis of agreement must involve justice to each, and such agreement is possible only when that mutual dependence is understood. Perhaps there is no place where brotherhood is more commonly disregarded than in the relation between the races. Race hatred and solidarity are mutually exclusive. The vision of the great sheet filled with diverse kinds of animals which came to Peter on the housetop has not lost its timeliness. It has often been cited as a warrant for foreign missions, but it also strikes much nearer home. It needs to be better understood that selfishness is not always a personal sin. Just as personal selfishness operates against the welfare of the group and ultimately against the person himself, so group selfishness is fatal in society and finally wrecks the group itself where it originated. A community or a nation can no more live to itself than can an individual. The operation of this law may be slow, but it is sure. It is well for each of us to think carefully at this point and not to be content with generalization. Let each remove the beam from his own eye before attempting to remove the mote from the eye of another. It is easier to say what labor and capital should do than to shape our own conduct. Scarcely one of us is free from the prejudice of habit in this matter.

The Christ Spirit must prevail.—The great challenge to Christian men and women to-day is to so think and live in every human relationship that the Christ spirit shall prevail. The tragedies of human existence appear where the Christ spirit is lacking. The materialistic philosophy of life, which so largely controls our thinking to-day, has nearly succeeded in convincing the world that a man's life does consist in the abundance of things which he possesseth. But where this thought holds sway divisive tendencies are always evidenced. The Christ spirit is unifying. The church sings, "We are not divided, all one body we," in complacent disregard of the facts. The Master's prayer with its petition, "Thy kingdom come, thy will be done," will sound out with new meaning in our churches when the spirit of Christ prevails over the narrow, sectarian spirit. Peace will come to the industrial world, justice and brotherliness will be working principles, and the dynamic of loving hearts will have a chance to operate when the spirit of Christ triumphs over the spirit of partisan and selfish class-consciousness. That ancient word that God "hath made of one blood all nations of men to dwell on all the face of the earth" will be realized when the spirit of Christ so controls that the ugly spirit of race hatred will be driven from the hearts of men.

EXERCISES

1. "Are comradeship and team work instinctive or must they be learned?" (Rauschenbusch.)
2. How long must a group be associated to gain class-consciousness?
3. Does the team spirit ever go wrong?
4. Give examples of where the principle of solidarity is acted upon in modern life. Also examples of its rejection.
5. Is a college fraternity fraternal?
6. Do church organizations help or hinder the realization of social solidarity?
7. Have you ever made an entirely original discovery?
8. Are your political convictions original or borrowed? Your religious beliefs?
9. Did Jesus need friends? Does he now?
10. How much of the model prayer is social and how much personal?
11. Give passages from the Gospels showing that Jesus regarded unity of spirit between persons as essential.
12. Did Jesus' ideas of solidarity extend beyond the Jewish race?
13. Name several social groups that exhibit the Christian spirit of solidarity.

14. Is love as a basis for race solidarity found in other than Christian sources?
15. Is the need for others an indication of strength or of weakness?
16. Consider some personal experiences of forgiving and of being forgiven; which had the more solidifying effect on your social relationship?
17. Do hatred and the unforgiving spirit disprove solidarity?

Topics for Further Discussion

1. The connection of love and solidarity.
2. Fraternity amd modern business.
3. Religion and social unity.
4. The Lord's Prayer and the spirit of solidarity.
5. The friendship of Jesus.
6. The strike in relation to human solidarity.

Suggested Readings

Rauschenbusch, *The Social Principles of Jesus*, Chapter II.
Fosdick, *The Manhood of the Master*, Study IX.

CHAPTER V

THE MASTER'S KINGDOM IDEALS

To appreciate the Master's ideals for his kingdom we must understand his viewpoint. As has been pointed out previously, while his acquaintance with life was intimate and detailed, he had for himself the comprehensive view. It is sometimes said that one fails to see the forest for the trees. The Master makes no such mistake.

The Master's attitude may be likened to that of the head of a great business concern who understands the need and use of trucks, and paper wrappings, and bills and bookkeeping. Such a man appreciates the value of details, and may be familiar with many of them from his own experience, but he is not bound by them. He outlines policies and expects others to carry them out. He considers world-wide trade movements, not profits on a single transaction, but still is not unmindful that success is built out of single successful transactions. Such an attitude lifts one away from the distortions of the too close view. Whatever the field, it seems almost impossible to combine familiarity concerning the intimate details with a broad comprehension of the whole plan. Such a "close-up" usually leads us to color the whole with the aspects of the local situation. For the leader the well-balanced, comprehensive grasp is vital.

This view of life is the view of clear vision and true perspective. The leader in social work must have it; he must see things in the large, and sometimes this will lead him to change his methods. Organized charity considers the need of a whole community, and so in a single case may need to pursue a different course than that which private sympathy would indicate. Dr. Stewart was mayor of a certain Michigan city when an epidemic of smallpox broke out. He was at once concerned with plans for quarantining and sanitation, and may possibly have given less attention to his private practice than he otherwise would have done. His duty as a public officer exceeded his responsibilities as a physician. Why did Christ denounce in such bitter terms the scribes and Pharisees? It was because they overlooked great things while gazing at little ones. They tithed mint and anise and cumin and neglected judgment, mercy, and faith. They had lost all sense of proportion and so were utterly unable to see clearly. It is precisely this remoteness and elevation of mind that enabled Jesus to speak so clearly and surely about social issues. "He only truly sees things who sees round them and beyond them. ... Sometimes it happens that the highest wisdom in affairs of the practical world is an endowment of the most unworldly men. They see into life by seeing over it."

The comprehensive view is the view of hope. The close view is often discouraging. We see, social unrest, unloving and unlovely men, greed, selfishness, political corruption, little children sacrificed to the demon of commercial advantage. We see Christian people indifferent, pleasure-seeking, ignorant, and far from following the life of service. Plans fail and success seems an utopian dream. It is a gloomy, discouraging outlook, and we need the hope of God in our hearts. But it is only the gloom of the too close view. As Dr. Mathews puts it, "He [the Christian] is not working desperately, uncertain of ultimate success. He is working with God and God must bring in his own kingdom."[1] The words of the Master are: "Fear not, little flock; for it is your Father's good pleasure to bring you the kingdom." This circumspective view has already been referred to as one of the elements of value in Christ's appraisal of life.

Having then considered his viewpoint, we are ready to ask what basic principles the Master gives us for the solution of the tangled problems of the social life. What are the ideals of the Kingdom? They may be comprised under three statements: the approach to life from within; the reclamation of social relations through service; the orientation of life with respect to God.

The approach to life from within.—When we remember the high estimate placed by the Master on the worth of the individual it will occasion no surprise to find that he regards the individual as the social unit. The first ideal of the Kingdom, then, is concerned with the individual and his inner, personal life. The transformation of social life is to take place by making vital changes in folks themselves. Jesus insists that the essential things are within, for it is from the heart that the issues of life proceed. He paints a vivid word picture, directs its moral toward the men of that generation who

[1] *The Social Gospel*, p. 29.

need it most, and pointedly shows that external whitewash can no more cover inner rottenness in the moral world than in the physical (Matthew 23: 25-28). It is not enough to polish life, it must be renovated throughout.

In our anxiety to move forward rapidly in great reforms, we sometimes forget this principle that to be lasting and effective social change must involve the individual. It takes sound timber to build a sound ship and it takes sound people to build a sound community. A right social order can no more be constructed of unsound folks than an army can be recruited from cripples or a college faculty from an insane asylum. Harnack says, "The gospel is not one of social improvement but one of spiritual redemption." It may be objected that these statements are directly opposed to the very proposition with which we started, that is, the social message of the gospel. On consideration it will be seen that such is not the case. The point is, rather, that the social message cannot possibly be vital unless it is deepseated in personal worth and achievement.

It seems, then, that the social gospel by no means neglects the personal regeneration of the individual, which fact some have feared the social emphasis might cause to be obscured. Rather it has retained and enriched the idea. "The most important religious insight, the insight requisite to the vitality of social religion and the success of our civilization, is the insight to discern that if the kingdom of God is to come in the earth, it must first come in our hearts. Social salvation can only be realized through individual salvation. The social awakening must be realized by a revival of personal religion."[2] We may well add that the kingdom of God can by no means come in our hearts unless in so doing it is also coming on earth. The major emphasis of the social gospel is on the rightness of the individual and of his environment. Individual regeneration and social regeneration are but two aspects of the same thing—but the two sides of the shield.

The reclamation of life through service.—Man has made a sad mess of social living. In his selfishness he has departed far from that ancient guiding principle that Jesus restated as the second great commandment. But to love one's neighbor is more than an emotion, something other than a state of mind. It implies helpful doing, as Jesus shows by his parable of the Jericho road. The Master's second great social principle is the reclamation of social relations through service. It is the logical outcome of the interest which Jesus has in the solidarity of the race. It means, as has already been said, that the saved individual must function socially, or, as James expressed it, must show his faith by his works. The changed life of the individual thus becomes manifest as a social force.

The parables of the Kingdom (Matthew 13: 1–52) clearly show the social nature of the kingdom of God and the leavening power of its gospel (Matthew 13: 24–50). "The field is the world." "The kingdom of heaven is like unto leaven." It grows from small beginnings as mustard springs from a tiny seed. In fact, the test of an individual's soundness (salvation) is his faithfulness to social duties (Matthew 25: 31–46). "The progress of Christian

---

[2] Finney, *Personal Religion and the Social Awakening*, p. 24.

society in the world will depend upon the power which each nucleus of Christian persons gathered into a society will have upon the surrounding social life."

This idea of service as a life principle is set forth by Jesus in many ways. Consider some of them. In the parable of the unfruitful fig tree (Luke 13:6–9) the issue is clear: be useful or be cut down. On another occasion the sons of Zebedee came to him eager to obtain preferment in the long-expected kingdom. They only knew one road to position— the favor of some one sitting in the place of power. Jesus quickly set them right and stated the conditions of greatness in his kingdom, as follows: "Whosoever will be great among you, let him be your minister; and whosoever will be chief among you, let him be your servant" (Matthew 20: 20–28). The good Samaritan has become an ideal of Christian charity because he turned aside to render needed service. The call to the discipleship was a call to service. The labors of the apostles were characterized by the spirit which Paul describes in these words: "Let no one be forever seeking his own good, but let each seek that of his fellow men" (1 Corinthians 10: 24). Almost the last word that came in the vision of Patmos to John the Aged was, "My reward is with me, that I may requite every man in accordance with what his conduct has been" (Revelation 22: 12).

It is an impressive fact that Jesus put himself under this same law of service. He asks nothing of his followers which he is not himself willing to do. He gave the disciples a vivid illustration by taking the place of a household servant and washing their stained feet. In the great high-priestly

prayer the guiding principle of his whole life is
expressed in the words, "For their sake I conse-
crate myself." Every moment of his life was an
expression of this. Sometimes the service took
humble form, ministering to physical needs such
as hunger or sick bodies. Again the soul thirst of
a Samaritan woman, or the intellectual need of a
Nicodemus was satisfied. The first miracle at Cana
was a helpful response to a human need. As day
after day the Master trod the weary miles over
dusty Judæan roads, there was unfolded a life of
service that reached its highest in the supreme
sacrifice on Calvary.

The orientation of life.—In the older days, when
a great cathedral was erected, care was taken to
have it properly orientated, that is to say, so placed
that the great altar should be in the eastern end of
the building. Peculiar efficacy was supposed to
be given to prayer when the petitioner faced the
rising sun. Having left behind the superstition
upon which such a custom rested, it is still well
for us to remember the value of a proper orientation
in a less literal sense. The physicists tell us that a
bar of iron is made up of minute elements, each a
tiny magnet. Their arrangement is irregular, some
pointing in one direction, some in another. Under
the influence of a magnetic field they rearrange
themselves so that they all point in one direction
and we say the iron bar has become magnetized.
There is no change in the parts, but only in their
direction, their arrangement. They have become
orientated to the magnetic field. Without attempting to apply these illustrations—imperfect at best—
too literally, they indicate this truth: that there

is an important factor in life besides the individual acts of which it is made up. The great relations are of importance also. It makes a difference which way we are headed, as well as what we are doing at the moment. Among these relations the one of supreme importance is that of the soul to God. It matters much that a man be filial, a good neighbor, and a loyal citizen. But it matters much more that he be at one with God; and, of course, if this latter be true, the lesser relations will follow. In fact, one cannot be in right relation with God and wrong in attitude toward his fellows.

One cannot read the Gospels and miss the one great master purpose of Jesus' life. It was to do his Father's will. That was not only his supreme purpose; it was his only purpose. From the visit to the Temple at twelve until Gethsemane's shadows gather round him "my Father's business" is his one concern. Read again John 5: 26–30; 36–38; 8: 28, 29; 12: 44–50; 14: 8–14 and 15: 9–10. In fact, the whole book of John reveals Jesus' consciousness of being at one with his Father. As Dr. Fosdick phrases it, "All his life is saturated with this consciousness of an incommunicable relationship with God, a unique union of life with the divine." It is also his ideal for his followers. It is not enough to follow externally the things Jesus said, we must also have the same driving motive, the passion to serve God. Here, then, is the secret of a right orientation with respect to God. It is precisely the same as the purpose of Jesus, to know and do the will of the Father. A familiar story told of President Lincoln illustrates this need and at the same time reveals the secret of the great liberator's power. At one of the times of severe strain during the war a friend came to him and said: "Mr. Lincoln, the Lord is with us. God is surely on our side in this great conflict." The answer of the President, gravely and quietly given, was this, "I am less anxious, friend, to know that the Lord is on our side than I am to make sure that we are on the Lord's side."

Exercises

1. What is meant by, "He only truly sees things who sees round them and beyond them."
2. How can it be explained that a State senator, himself a kind father, should vote against a child-labor law?
3. Why is a close-up view in social service often discouraging?
4. Point out essential differences in Christ's estimate of the social life of his time and the view of the Pharisees.
5. Why could not an ideal community be expected in a convict colony? What would be its defects?
6. How large a proportion of the population may be morally unsound without social risk to the community?
7. Give an original example of the social risk in individual unsoundness.
8. Name some forces which are social safeguards operating upon individuals.
9. Are there any social problems which can be solved without the individual approach?
10. Give examples of social change through service.
11. Interpret the parable of the leaven.

12. Explain the significance of the Prince of Wales' motto, "Ich dien."
13. Is the ideal of service peculiarly a Christian one?
14. Which is more important, the "act" or the "motive" of social helpfulness?
15. Name five institutions of modern life, dominated by the ideal of unselfish service. Five that violate it.
16. How far did Jesus' consciousness of a peculiar relationship with God affect his views of human life?
17. Does one's personal attitude toward God affect his power as a social worker?

Topics for Further Study

1. The evangelistic message of the social gospel.
2. Does the remote attitude of some social workers toward the church result in loss of sympathy on their part?
3. The regeneration of ancient society through service.
4. Jesus' conception of the Kingdom.
5. Will the readjustments of social life be hastened by applying the motives of religion to them?
6. May we expect the Kingdom ever to be fully established?

Suggested Readings

Mathews, *The Social Gospel*, Chapter II.
Rauschenbusch, *Christianizing the Social Order*, Part 2.
Taylor, *Religion in Social Action*, Chapter I.
Batten, *The Social Task of Christianity*, Chapter III.
Kent, *The Social Teachings of the Prophets and Jesus*, Chapters XVI, XVII, XVIII.
Finney, *Personal Religion and the Social Awakening*, Chapter II.

CHAPTER VI

A NEW DYNAMIC

JESUS' program of social reconstruction was indicated in the preceding chapter. It is very simply stated, involving but three points; the personal approach to life from within, the reclamation of social relations through service, the orientation of life with respect to God. These are not to be regarded as consecutive steps, but, rather, as three, phases of a single process. Men who have learned to draw upon the infinite source of power are shaping their environment and controlling their inner living to conformity with Kingdom ideals. There is no elaborate propaganda, no machinery of organization, just a simple message spoken to a few followers and left in their hearts to do its work. Much of the secret of this simplicity, and much of its power as well, is to be found in the Master's true scale of values. Jesus did not disregard possessions or amusements or food or any other of the many life values, but he did invariably put them in right relation to each other and to the higher values. He saw that much of our difficulty comes from trying to have mutually exclusive things. God and mammon cannot both have first place. Jesus revised the current scales of values in many ways. The religionists had burdened the observance of the Sabbath with a multitude of petty rules which quite overshadowed its spiritual values. It was a most surprising reversal to them to have Jesus insist that man is of more importance than any institution, even a time-honored religious custom (Mark 2: 27). The Oriental idea that power and position were to be used for personal gain was firmly fixed in that day, but the Master substituted service as the badge of greatness.

The world needs sorely to learn this lesson. Social confusions would largely disappear and life be wonderfully simplified if we could see all things in their true proportions—put first things first. Society had gone on insisting that might is greater than right, that property is more worth while than folks, that money outweighs brains, that a majority is always right, until these and scores of other fallacies have become its "practical" working rules. True, some ancient lies, like the divine right of kings, have been laid aside, but many more need to go to the scrap-heap. If we could but catch the Master's singleness of vision and his sensitiveness to moral values, then his program of social life would more easily be adopted.

The simplicity of the Master's method.—Contrast this simplicity of method with the elaborate but incomplete plans of man's contriving. Think of three examples taken from widely separated periods of history. Plato's republic, where the philosophers were to rule, sought the virtue and happiness of the individual citizen. Division of labor, exact laws for the selection of the rulers, the limitation of the population into various groups were among the plans proposed to overcome the recognized weaknesses of social groups of that time. Two thousand years later Sir Thomas More wrote "Utopia," a romance of a happy society on an imaginary island. This ideal contemplated a society where none should be idle and none overworked. Happiness and the common good was to be the goal of all. To this end there were proposed community of property interests, gold and silver used for baser vessels only, freedom in religion and only such laws as were absolutely needed and could be understood by any reader. Modern socialism exhibits a wide diversity of applications of its relatively simple fundamentals. In all its ramifications of state socialism, socialists of the chair, right and left wings, Fabians, Utopians, and other varieties are developed many methods of meeting social needs. The final outcome, however, is the same, a complete revamping of society so that the maladjustments now present may be avoided. Numerous other programs for social improvement might be mentioned which would differ in practicality and method. Each of these would provide in multiplied detail for the many phases of life. In their incomplete complexity they are in striking contrast with the simple completeness of the plan of Jesus.

However, though the program is simple, its purpose is amazing—nothing less indeed than the transformation of the world. The note of this tremendous project was first sounded in prophecy: "He hath sent me to bind up the broken-hearted, to proclaim liberty to the captives, ... to comfort all that mourn." Christ himself had the vision clearly, for he adds after reading these words in the synagogue: "To-day is this scripture fulfilled in your hearing." Many men have had the vision of world-conquest—Alexander and Napoleon and Wilhelm, for example—but their notion of conquest was to bend the nations to their will, to acquire power, to establish themselves. Self-interest was at the center of their universe. But here was one who thought in terms of brotherhood and helpfulness to others. In the very humanity of Jesus' program its transcendent greatness has often been missed. "Come unto me, all ye that labor and are heavy laden, and I will give you rest," seems too simple a formula for world-transformations. The fact remains that Jesus' life and teachings released the most potent force the world has known. This consideration should give new meaning to those words in Luke 17: 20, "The kingdom of God cometh not with observation," or, as Weymouth suggests, The kingdom of God does not so come that you can keep close to it and watch it as outsiders.

A new insight into life.—This transformation of life has two aspects. There is the overcoming of evil which, as we have seen, is a process affecting both the personal life and instincts and also the social relations and institutions. Its ultimate aim is the elimination of wrong and unsocial impulses and the correction of conditions which have come out of such impulses. Then there is the at least equally important constructive result that life is given a new objective. In fact, to merely clean out the old without replacing it with new and better things may result in great disaster. Remember Jesus' parable of the seven spirits: "No sooner has the foul spirit gone out of the man than he roams about in places where there is no water, seeking rest but finding none. Then he says, 'I will return to my house that I left'; and he comes and finds it unoccupied, swept clean and in good order. Then he goes and brings back with him seven other spirits more wicked than himself, and they come in and dwell there; and in the end that man's condition becomes worse than it was at first."[1]

So it is essential that not only shall the uncomfortable and evil things of life be removed, but that also a soul-satisfying vision shall be given. "This transfiguration of common life is what Jesus offers to men in his vision of the kingdom of God. He looks upon the striving, struggling world of social movement as contributing to that social intention. He sees the

> . . . one far off, divine event,
> To which the whole creation moves.

Neither the turbulence of the stream, nor its reactionary eddies, make him forget the ocean to which it flows. The pettiness, the toil, the routine, the insignificance of life—even its pain and bitterness —are swept into the movement of his mighty hope, and become a part of its greatness instead of an obstacle to its course. Thus the teaching of Jesus gives meaning to many an obscure life, caught in the perplexity of the modern world. It offers to such a life, not first of all *a new set of circumstances*, but a new *insight* into and through its circumstances."[2]

Right here appears the essential unlikeness of

---

[1] Matthew 12: 43–45.
[2] Peabody, *Jesus Christ and the Social Question*, p. 120. The Macmillan Company.

Jesus' social program to every other. They deal primarily with detailed methods and readjustments. He puts first an adequate motive. The things which men should do are not so hard to define. They have been often stated, but what power is great enough to make them do these things? The machinery is all here, but where is the steam to run it? The master power, the new dynamic which Jesus proposes, is Christian love. It is the keynote of the gospel message, for when the Master was asked to indicate the greatest commandment, he replied, "Thou shalt love the Lord thy God with all thy heart, and with all thy soul, and with all thy mind, . . . and thy neighbor as thyself."[3] One great law of love; two objects—God and fellow man. Again, in John 15: 12, we read, "This is my commandment, that ye love one another." And the apostle writes: "Ye yourselves are taught of God to love one another."[4] This is a new emphasis on love, for while it was present in a secondary way in the old law, Christ raised it to the place of preeminence.

The dynamic power of love.—Christian love is more than mere affection. Dr. Francis has defined it as "intelligent good will toward all mankind raised to the degree of passion." Love is always something other than liking. It is possible to love those whom one cannot like. A few days ago a poor lad sat in my office. He had been caught stealing from his fellow students. Investigation proved him to be a thief, a liar, guilty of immorality, a "dope" user—and now to be expelled from college.

[3] Matthew 22: 37–39.
[4] Thessalonians 4: 9.

One can hardly picture the emotions of his mother, in her home in an Eastern State, when she finally hears, as she must, the story of her son's degradation. She will find little to like in that wayward boy, but can we doubt that she will still love him? This thought that love does not depend upon liking is very significant in understanding the nature of Christian love and the possibility of obeying the Master's injunction to love one's enemies. The apostle tells us that "Love is patient and kind. Love knows neither envy nor jealousy. Love is not forward and self-assertive; . . . she finds no pleasure in injustice done to others, but joyfully rides with the truth" (1 Corinthians 13:4, 6). These are not merely the marks by which love is to be recognized. They are intrinsic parts of its spirit, inevitable results of the will of love. It is a mistake to regard Christian love as just an affair of the emotions and dependent upon the ebb and flow of feelings. Sometimes the will must command. I must be "Captain of my soul," and say, "Thus shalt thou act." Then Christian love is in control, base motives are put down, fine instincts released, brotherhood achieved, and God honored.

There is a good deal of talk about the brotherhood of man. It might be well to talk less and practice it more. Christian love is the only enduring basis for such fraternity, for then it rings true and is not perfunctory nor condescending. Jesus expects such fraternity to exist among his followers, for he says, "All ye are brethren." Fraternal love is by no means the only kind of love, for a master may love a slave or an inferior his superior. But among the disciples of Jesus there is to be no exercising of lordship one over another, so that fraternal love with its leveling effect is to prevail.

"But this noble truth of the fraternity of those who are children of God cannot be limited in its practical working simply to the church. It is true that it would be overlooking certain fundamental differences to say that the man who persists in sin is equal to the man in whom the Spirit of God is really living. For sin is the great unequalizing force in society, and one of its most persistent forces is selfishness, and selfishness consists in making one's own advantages superior to those of other people. But the Christian cannot treat those who treat him unfraternally in any spirit but that of fraternity. The attitude of the elder brother toward the prodigal can never be his so long as he trusts the impulses of the Christian experience. Whether it be in the family or in politics or in business, this principle of Jesus must always be operative. True, the Christian is not to cast his pearls before swine, but he is not to treat other people in any way different from that in which he would like to be treated himself. Thus, in whatever sphere he may act, whether it be in his capacity as citizen, as husband, or as a neighbor, he will bring into social life this fraternal spirit. That is the only possible meaning of the "Golden Rule."[5]

The history of punishment as a means of enforcing justice is a long and interesting one which can but be hinted at here. In early times punishment was left in the hands of the wronged person or his friends, and so more than frequently partook of the nature of revenge. It is a long road from this

[5] Mathews, *The Social Gospel*, pp. 27, 28.

custom, which made necessary "Cities of Refuge," to the theories of modern criminology which consider punishment as remedial and corrective in character. A feeble logic has sometimes thought that since God is love he, therefore, cannot punish. Human experience in almost any family should teach us that love sometimes *must* punish. But this is what love can do: it can save justice from the danger of degenerating into revenge. It can make people kind even while they are strictly just. So it will be found that love has an ennobling power over all human relations. Even when they are necessarily rigorous, as in the example just given, the saving human touch is possible. Justice may be tempered with mercy and yet lose no whit of its power.

Here, then, lies the real difference between Christianity and other social plans. They all propose justice, the square deal, honesty, fraternity—they set up perfectly good machinery, but lack a propulsive force, a dynamic. The driving force which Jesus proposes is love. It is an expulsive force driving a man out of the narrow, selfish limits of his own life. A heart energized by the love of God and living in a loving fashion toward others is the hope of society.

EXERCISES

1. Give an example of social confusion arising from a false scale of values.
2. Give two illustrations of a reversal made by Jesus in scales of values current in his day.
3. What were the main proposals of Plato's Republic?

4. Explain: "There are two ways to be contented; to have what you want and to want what you have."

5. Can all "pain and bitterness" of life be removed by obtaining a new insight into life?

6. Name some of the dynamics of life—the things which impel men to divers lines of action. Which of these are social and which anti-social in results? Would the substitution of the word "Christian" for "social" in the above question cause you to change your answer?

7. What results would follow the application of the principle of Christian love:
   (a) to child labor.
   (b) to sectarian disputes.
   (c) to our attitude toward other races.
   (d) to commercialized amusements.

8. What are the essentials of true fraternal feeling?

9. Do college fraternities promote fraternity?

10. Is love incompatible with justice? Why do they sometimes appear to be in conflict?

11. Does the exercise of Christian love involve sacrifice?

12. Is the element of revenge ever present in our punishment of criminals?

13. Give an example of change in a social attitude due to the action of Christian love.

14. Do the following things help or hinder the individual in following the law of love in his social relations?
    (a) A college education.
    (b) Membership in a church.
    (c) Belonging to a fraternal order.
    (d) The competition of business.
    (e) Foreign travel.

15. "If a man loved his enemies and turned the other cheek, would he be everybody's doormat or everybody's friend and refuge?" (Rauschenbusch.)

TOPICS FOR FURTHER STUDY

1. Jesus' life as an example of sacrificial love.
2. The Golden Rule as a business principle.
3. The comprehensive simplicity of the gospel of living.
4. Modern society's impediments to a love-governed life.
5. The God of law is a God of love.
6. The place of love in the Mosaic law.

SUGGESTED READINGS

Mathews, *The Social Gospel*, Chapter III.

Mathews, *The Gospel and the Modern Man*, Chapter V.

Peabody, *Jesus Christ and the Social Question*, Chapter II.

Rauschenbusch, *Christianizing the Social Order*, pp. 47–68.

CHAPTER VII

IS THERE PROGRESS?

The gospel of Jesus has an individualistic message with a social outreach. It proposes to transform human society by the brotherly actions of people whose hearts have been renewed. Its simple law is that one should do unto others as he would have others do unto him. The dynamic which is to bring this to pass is the power of Christian love. Jesus left this gospel resident in the hearts of a few disciples and trusted to its expulsive force to transform the world. He placed a little yeast in a very great lump and expressed his satisfaction in the words, "I have finished the work which thou gavest me to do."[1] Has this transformation taken place? Is the lump at all leavened? Is our present-day social order Christian? What is a Christian social order? When is a given social institution Christian? These are some of the questions which come promptly to mind as we think of the social ends contemplated by the program of Jesus. Before attempting to indicate a method of approach to these questions let us consider some of the reasons for believing that these social benefits are indeed contemplated in the world-plan which Jesus proposed.

Social change the plan of the Master.—*The social*

[1] John 17: 4.

nature of the duties enjoined upon his followers is the primary reason. This has already been somewhat fully discussed in preceding chapters. A full catalogue of these social duties is unnecessary; some of them may be mentioned which will indicate the wide scope of Jesus' expectations for his followers. They are to be charitable and render helpful service to those in need (Luke 10: 30–37; Matthew 5: 1–4). Hatred and revenge are to be put aside (Matthew 5: 22, 38–40) and purity of life and thought sought for (Matthew 5: 28, 29). Humility is commended (Matthew 18: 1–5) and a forgiving spirit enjoined (Matthew 18: 21, 22). In short, the Christian is to be a better father, a truer husband, and a nobler citizen and neighbor than he would without the Spirit of God in his heart.

The Christianizing of the social order was the very aim with which Christianity started. Our information about the early church is meager, obtained mainly from the book of Acts and the Epistles. Furthermore, what expressions are found there are modified by two important considerations. One is the hampering effect of the Roman rule. The idea of social change and improvement would have been a very dangerous one to talk much about, and it is not strange that little is said concerning it in the Epistles. To have attacked slavery, political corruption, and public graft would have been to expose the church to even more severe peril than already threatened it. Again, it must always be remembered that during that period there was expected the immediate return of the Lord to set up his kingdom, when all these things would come about as a matter of course. This latter attitude

has not disappeared yet, for there are to-day some
people so concerned with the probable date of this
second coming that they have no time for some very
evident present duties. A minister in a neighboring
town said, "I have no interest in social betterment.
Jesus will take care of that when he comes."

In spite of these two circumstances, however, a
study of the early church reveals its social vision.
One evidence of this is that the social teachings of
Jesus were embodied in the Gospels. These books
were all written many years after his death and
record the things which seemed of major importance
to the authors. It is, therefore, significant and
indicative of the attitude of the early Christians
that these social sayings are preserved. Again, other
evidence is found in the organization of the early
churches and Christian communities. They provided for the common religious worship, but at
least equally important was the provision for mutual
helpfulness. In charity, for example, there was an
open-handedness which gave the church such a
start in this direction that it has been the chief
charitable agency throughout the centuries. "This
fraternal helpfulness was more than mere religious
kindliness. It was animated by the consciousness
of a creative social mission and accompanied by a
spirit of social unrest which proves the existence of
powerful currents of democratic feeling. Under
the first impact of its ideas and spirit, men and
women tried to realize at once those social changes
which have actually been accomplished in centuries
of development."[2]

With the passing years the church ceased to be

[2] *Christianity and the Social Crisis*, p. 141. The Macmillan Company.

a fugitive band and came to a position of great power. Its organization was developed and its leaders became concerned with discussions of doctrine and involved in politics. How, with this growth in popularity, the original social ideal was obscured and nearly lost is beyond the limits of this discussion. This is, however, exactly what happened, and the present generation is witnessing a return of interest and the "rebirth of the social hope."[3] The return to the original conception of the kingdom of God as a wonderful, present possibility, and not simply a glorious future hope, will necessitate new thinking, new action, and perhaps new theology for great sections of Christendom. Consider, for example, the hymnals. How small and meager the sections devoted to hymns of service and social vision! New hymns, new prayers, and new creeds will be needed to define the goals and express the purposes of the Kingdom that is here and now.

The individualist's objections.—The position indicated in the preceding paragraphs is by no means the unanimous view of Christian people to-day. There are those who very radically and very sincerely disagree with it. No one doubts that the transformation of individual lives is one result of the teachings of Jesus. Will the application of these teachings also result in changing society, in remaking human institutions? There are some people who do not think so; they do not believe that the ideas of righteousness found in the Sermon on the Mount will really ever operate among nations or in social life. They believe in the moral life of

[3] For a helpful discussion of this loss of the social ideal see *Christianizing the Social Order*, Part 2, Chapters II, III, and IV.

individuals but not of the social group. To such people the kingdom of God is not a present possibility but a future hope to be realized either in another world or through a new dispensation in this one. The Scriptures seem to them to teach that there is no hope of progress and that "everything is to become as Sodom and Gomorrah."

Perhaps the best answer to this is that "there can be no complete salvation of the individual apart from the heavenly kingdom; there can be no process of working out our salvation with God's help, except we bring God into increasing control of the politics, the industry, the domestic life of the world. Such control can never be absolute as long as sin is in society, but it can be made ever more complete. Such a conception to the practical politician may seem an iridescent dream, but to the Christian it is sober reality. It is the call of Christ's spirit in all Christians to bring these ideals of Jesus into social life. . . . Thus, though it is true, as has already been said, that the Christlike individual is the final goal of all progress, it is just as true that such an individual is impossible except in connection with the kingdom of God."[4] Now, this does not mean that an individual may not attempt to live the Christian life amid unchristian surroundings. In fact, such attempts are rather frequently and successfully made. What Dr. Mathews would point out is that completeness of Christian experience is normally possible only within the Kingdom; that is, it is possible only to the one who is surrounded by others who are striving in the same direction.

[4] Mathews, *The Social Gospel*, pp. 21, 22.

The attitude of many of those who hold this "individualistic" view is rather well expressed by a certain type of hymn such as:

> "Traveling through a barren land
> O'er the desert's scorching sand."

Earth is a place to be escaped from, human society is a snare, the church a place of temporary refuge for weary pilgrims. Bunyan's allegory of escape from the City of Destruction and an anxious pressing on to the Celestial City seems to them a complete picture of the Christian life. The totality of the gospel message is to them a personal salvation, an escape from future punishment and an avenue to future bliss. Quite naturally and logically the business of the church is felt to be the "snatching of brands from the burning." As has already been brought out, the hope of social regeneration does not minimize, still less abandon, the need of personal salvation. On the contrary, it rests its hope of social soundness on the integrity of the individual. Where the one who holds this view differs from the "individualist" is in the functioning of this saved life. He believes that the gospel of justice and mercy and love will work and that the Kingdom will be established among men. When such a one uses the Lord's Prayer he says, "Thy kingdom come, thy will be done on earth as it is in heaven," with the conviction that such an outcome is his Master's will and desire and that he wishes each of his followers to whole-heartedly work for its fulfillment.

Testing the social order.—Let us now return to the consideration of the questions proposed about the institutions of social life. What is a Christian social order? When is a given social institution Christian? The term "Christian" has come to be used rather loosely, and we speak of Christian notions, Christian ideals, a Christian civilization, etc., with little real intent to define these things as conforming to the ideals of Christ. In the careless thought of the street all is Christian that is not pagan. It is in the more restricted and truer sense of the word that we use it here, and the inquiry is about likeness to the ideals and teaching of Jesus the Christ. To arrive at this, four tests may be proposed.

First. *See if it conforms to the actual and specific teaching of Jesus concerning it.* Where this is possible it is, of course, the most certain and satisfactory test that can be used. When Jesus makes a direct statement, as about the permanence of the marriage relation for example, there can be no doubt as to the Christian standard. It is conceivable that men might reject the teaching, might question its value, or neglect its application, but certainly the authority of Christ to state the conditions for Christian living cannot be disputed. Christians might easily fail to agree upon standards of action, as they have done so often. The church may be mistaken in its positions, but surely the founder of Christianity will have an authoritative note when he chooses to sound it. These direct statements will often be quite explicit, in other cases less so and upon many subjects Jesus will be entirely silent. Relatively speaking, these specific teachings will be few although clear and definite when they do occur.

Second. *Consider the incidental teaching found in*

other connections. Frequently while talking about some matter the Master throws a strong light on something else. Thus the parable of the Good Samaritan was spoken to illustrate the command quoted just previously about loving one's fellow men. Incidentally, it furnishes an excellent program of poor relief. These less direct teachings are of great value and are to be carefully considered.

Third. *Does it agree with the general ideals of the Kingdom?* The conclusions reached in this way will be quite as final, but more difficult of attainment. It is much easier for a surgeon examining recruits for the army to find a man's height and weight than to say whether or not he is in good health. Estimating the number of correct answers in an examination paper in algebra is much simpler than determining the student's knowledge of the principles involved. One may keep all the Ten Commandments in form and still be unethical, unloving, and unchristian in spirit. Nevertheless, this third test is one of great importance! The fundamental life principles of the gospel are so far-reaching that human character and social institutions in their entirety may be rested upon them. When Jesus says, "Love your neighbor," the understanding of love and the defining of one's neighbor may take time and careful thought. Paul's definition of love as "the greatest of these" is more than a fine phrase; it is a just estimate of the potential power of a right principle.

Fourth. *Does the institution or custom help or hinder man's highest development?* So sure are we of the good will of Jesus' gospel that this test may be depended upon. In a sense this test includes all the others.   Jesus' utterances are not true just because he says them.   Rather he says them because they are true.   The word of Allah is law to the Mussulman because it is his word, not because of inherent truth.   It is an Oriental conception of despotic rulership.   God through Jesus expresses the truth which is His eternal nature.

The method of procedure will then be something like this.   First, an investigation to give familiarity with the actual conditions of social life. A knowledge of the gospel message must also be had.   Then there may be made an estimate of the conformity of conditions with the gospel standards. Perhaps the method will not always follow these three steps in a formal fashion, but certainly they must always be included eventually.   In the following chapters the method will be used in a few cases with the hope that it will suggest a fruitful field for further study.

We shall not find any human institution free from fault or wholly Christianized.   Even the church fails to measure up to standard, and so ancient and so fine a thing as the family falls short when placed beside the simple but lofty ideals of Jesus.   On the other hand, there will be few, if any, of the expressions of human life that are wholly bad.   The most hopeful thing that may be expected is progress, for it is true that where we stand still we go backward.   This progress may not be always easy to see.   Oftentimes the comparison must be made over pretty long intervals to be sure of the actual movement.   The surface ripples and waves do not always tell the direction of the tide; it is the deep under-surface movement that counts.

There is too the necessity of seeing clearly the sources of social change. When improvement is found a great interest attaches to the question "Why?" What has been the driving force that has brought about the change? There will be the temptation to overestimate the work of the church, to complacently assume credit which is not deserved. On the other hand, it not unfrequently happens that the effect of Christian teaching is discredited. The laxness and ineptitude of the church are noted and the readiness of other agencies credited, without remembering that they have their roots deep in the church and its influence. Whatever may be found about the various agencies, this much will be surely seen: that the gospel of Jesus Christ is the mighty power back of social improvement. Place the second century beside the twentieth and the contrast will appear. Put Christian lands over against non-Christian, or study the changes that follow the preaching of the gospel in heathen darkness, and the transforming power of the Good News is seen.

EXERCISES

1. Give evidence that the world is growing better.
2. What is the most nearly Christian of our social institutions? Which is the least so?
3. Quote two statements of Jesus, indicating the social purpose of his teaching.
4. Give four duties of a social nature which Jesus expects of his disciples.
5. Is it true that "A Christlike individual is impossible except in connection with the kingdom of God"?
6. What evidence can you find in the book of

Acts concerning the social nature of the early church?

7. Is there any incompatibility between a conviction that the gospel has a social significance and a belief in the second coming of Christ?

8. What direct teachings of Jesus about specific social problems can you recall?

9. What things would you consider to be included under "man's highest development"?

10. What new moral standards should result from the economic change of the last century?

11. Transportation has been revolutionized in the last century. Give some moral standards between nations and races which have been revised as a result.

12. "Does human nature welcome a moral advance?"

13. Do young people or old contribute most to advancing moral standards?

TOPICS FOR FURTHER STUDY

1. The family in 1920 and in the first century.
2. Personal Christianity as dependent on environment.
3. The church as a social agency.
4. The social activities of the apostolic church.
5. Intellectual advance and moral standards.
6. Modern-day Pharisees.

SUGGESTED READINGS

Batten, *The Social Task of Christianity*, Chapter IV.

Rauschenbusch, *Christianizing the Social Order*, Part 2, Chapters II and III; *Christianity and the Social Crisis*, Chapter III.

Finney, *Personal Religion and the Social Awakening*, Chapter I.

PART TWO

SOME PRACTICAL APPLICATIONS OF THE GOSPEL'S TEACHING

"We may dream and exult ever so much over a world growing better, but unless we can somehow bring social service down into close contact with the details of our lives and actually live by it as a motive, one of two things will happen: we shall either grow discouraged at the futility of our lives, or else we shall abstract our religion from our lives, praying and singing and exulting over a Kingdom-dream that we can only dream about, while meantime our daily lives are prayerless, visionless, and godless."[1]

In the preceding seven chapters some of the social implications of Jesus' teachings have been indicated. Starting with the essentially moral quality of all the problems of the social order, those ideals of the Kingdom were examined in which it is proposed to find a solution for these problems. These ideals rest upon the worth of the individual and the solidarity of the human family. The next section will be given to a more careful examination of the second of these ideals, the reclamation of social relations through service. What changes would take place in the various social institutions if all men should act under the impulse of love?

In chapter seven a method was suggested to be used in testing social procedure for Christian idealism. In the next few chapters the attempt will be made to use this method in specific cases. Of necessity this study cannot be at all complete. If, however, some lines of thought are suggested, and especially if interest in further and more careful study is stimulated, the writer's purpose will be met.

---

[1] Finney, *Personal Religion and the Social Awakening*, pp. 22, 23.

CHAPTER VIII

THE FAMILY

PROBABLY the most ancient of all our social institutions is the family; certainly it is one of the most important. It has sometimes been defined as the social unit. It is the only social institution which is universal in its touch upon the human kind, for every one sustains family relationships at some time.

Divorce.—In studying the family one soon discovers the growing tendency toward instability in the marriage relation. Divorce is a world-wide evil and on the increase. Among civilized nations the United States has the unenviable record of leading in the number of separations. "In the year 1905, for example, there were 20,000 more marriages legally dissolved in the United States than in all the rest of the Christian civilized world put together. In that year in France one marriage was legally dissolved to every thirty marriage ceremonies performed; in Germany, only one marriage was legally dissolved to every forty-four marriage ceremonies performed; in England, only one marriage legally dissolved to every four hundred marriage ceremonies performed. But in the United States the proportion was about one to twelve."[1] Furthermore, it is estimated that in this

[1] Bogardus, *Introduction to Sociology*, p. 66. The University of Southern California Press.

country the number of divorces is increasing three times as fast as the population.

The following tabulation has been compiled from the United States Census reports for 1916. The figures show the number of marriages per 100,000 population, the number of divorces per 100,000 and the ratio of marriages to divorces:

COUNTRY	MARRIAGES				DIVORCES				MARRIAGES TO ONE DIVORCE			
	1890	1900	1906	1916	1890	1900	1906	1916	1890	1900	1906	1916
United States...	910	930	1,020	1,050	53	73	84	112	17	13	12	9
Austria........	750	820	..	...	3	6	..	.	275	137	..	..
Belgium.......	730	860	790	. .	6	10	13		122	86	..	..
France.........	700	770	770	..	17	20	28	.	61	38	28	..
Great Britain...	780	800	760	. .	2	2	2		390	400	380	
Hungary.......	820	890	840	...	7	11	18	..	117	81	47	..

N. B.—The figures for all countries except the United States are for 1905 instead of 1906.

Something of the relative situations between the various States is shown by this comparison of the ratios of divorces to 100,000 population:

YEAR	HIGHEST RATIO		LOWEST RATIO	
1890....	Colorado...........	197	North Carolina......	12
1900....	Washington.........	184	Delaware...........	16
1906....	Washington.........	220	North Carolina......	18
1916....	Nevada.............	607	District of Columbia..	13

These ratios are, of course, affected by the varying stringency of the divorce laws in the different States. Perhaps most of the large number recorded against Nevada were dissolutions of marriages performed elsewhere. The inevitable result of legally dissolving so many marriages annually is an unstable condition of the family. Various causes are suggested for this instability. Among them may be mentioned (1) the decay of religion, (2) an increased spirit of individualism, (3) the industrial "emancipation" of women, (4) subnormal housing conditions, (5) late marriage, (6) laxness of divorce laws. It would seem, however, that none of these alleged causes are truly fundamental. They may be important contributory sources, but they in turn root down into substantial changes in the ideals of marriage and the home. Much of this has come through the gradual surrender by the home of its various social functions.

In more primitive times, when the family was isolated and social agencies were less developed, the functions of the family were much more varied. Sanitary measures, hospitals, and doctors have replaced the family medicine shelf. The police force and the fire department are depended upon for protection. Barter and exchange and manufacture are no longer carried on by the family group. Education, including training in trade technic, politics, morals, and religion, has been turned over to the school and the church. Of all the original functions of the family there is only one, reproduction, which has not been socialized to a greater or less degree. This has inevitably lessened the influence of the family on its members and lowered its stability. Contrast the situation of the farm lad of former times with the city boy of to-day. The former grew up in the house where his father and, perhaps, his grandfather had lived; ate food grown upon the place and wore clothes prepared from its wool and woven on its loom. He conned his lessons at the old fireplace, discussed religion and politics with his brothers, and performed his part of the common tasks. His modern brother has his attention directed away from the rented, temporary abode called home at almost every turn. Food and clothes come from the town stores. He studies at the school and worships, if at all, at the neighborhood church. His contact with industry is in shop or office. The newspaper and club and movie again wean him from home. These changes, desirable as many of them are, have tended to shift the emphasis from the group to the individual.

The entrance of women into industry has been an important factor also. It is obvious that home-making cannot be successfully accomplished by one who is seldom in the home, as is the case where the mother must work to supplement the husband's earnings. Again, the self-supporting young woman is loath to give up her good income, and late marriage often results. So far has this change gone in some instances as to lead Göhre to remark: "For a large part of the working population of our great industrial cities (Germany) the traditional form of the family no longer exists." From these and similar considerations some socialists have confidently predicted the passing of the family. It, with capitalism and religion, are regarded as forming the bulwarks of that social order whose overthrow is sought.

So we find these various active enemies of the family to-day—instability in the marriage relation, socialization of family functions, changed conditions in industry, and the disregard of some social

teachers. To these might well be added a lessen-
ing of parental authority, greater liberty between
the sexes, and a general revision of the ideals of the
home. A solution has been sought in various ways;
through legislation, through a revival of emphasis
on the teachings of the church, etc. "In these practical efforts for domestic integrity, however, there
is in reality involved a much larger issue than at
first appears. It is, in fact, nothing less than an
issue between two theories of the marriage tie—
the conception of it as a temporary contract involving the interests of those who are known as 'the
parties concerned,' and the conception of it as a
social institution involving the fabric of the social
order. Indeed, the family is but one element in a
general struggle for existence of two types of civilization, one dominated by an interest in the development of the individual, the other characterized
by a concern for the social order."[2]

Gospel ideals of marriage.—From this very
incomplete picture of the family let us turn to the
gospel and seek what word Jesus has on this subject. This will be found to be very definite—much
more so than in connection with most specific
social problems. Matthew records these words in
the nineteenth chapter, verses 3 to 9 (Weymouth
Version): "Then came some of the Pharisees to
Him to put Him to the proof by the question,

" 'Has a man a right to divorce his wife whenever he chooses?'

" 'Have you not read,' He replied, 'that He who
made them "MADE THEM" from the beginning

[2] Peabody, *Jesus Christ and the Social Question*, p. 131. The
Macmillan Company.

"MALE AND FEMALE (Gen. i. 27), AND SAID, FOR
THIS REASON A MAN SHALL LEAVE HIS FATHER AND
MOTHER AND BE UNITED TO HIS WIFE, AND THE TWO
SHALL BE ONE" (Gen. ii. 24)? Thus they are no
longer two, but "one"! What therefore God has
joined together, let not man separate.'

" 'Why then,' said they, 'did Moses command
the husband to give her "a written notice of divorce," and so put her away (Deut. xxiv. 1)?'

" 'Moses,' He replied, 'in consideration of the
hardness of your nature, permitted you to put
away your wives; but it has not been so from the
beginning. And I tell you that whoever divorces
his wife for any reason except her unfaithfulness,
and marries another woman, commits adultery.' "

(See also Mark 10: 2-12 and Luke 16: 18.)

These passages indicate that marriage is to be
permanent like other family relations. The fact
that it is entered into voluntarily while the others
are not makes no difference. We feel that only an
unnatural father will disown his own child no matter
how wayward it may become. The family ties between parents and children and between brothers
and sisters are not dissolved at will. This same
natural permanence is, according to Christ's teaching, to characterize the relation between husband
and wife. Divorce is not to be considered except,
possibly, for unchastity, and even this exception
is not mentioned by Mark or Luke. The teaching
may be unwelcome, but it certainly is not obscure;
one might feel with Renan that it is "overstrained
morality," but assuredly it is not equivocal.

It should be noted that this teaching does not,
as is sometimes contended, impose the burden of

continuing an uncomfortable and unholy relationship. It condemns no wife to a life of misery with
some selfish wretch of a husband. It condones no
continuance of a wedlock from which love has
departed. Separation is possible, but remarriage is
forbidden. A mistake in such an important matter
as this must needs carry with it a heavy burden.
As usual Jesus here struck at the very root of the
matter. Many a divorce case would never have
been considered except for the possible and in most
cases the probable remarriage. The Master is not
simply concerned with the adjustment of marital
difficulties; he is striking more deeply and reaching
the very source of many of these troubles. "It is
against the provoking of alienation by this antici-
pation of remarriage that Jesus makes his special
protest; and the modern world, with its voluntary
desertions often suggested by antecedent and ille-
gitimate affection, knows well how grave a social
peril it is with which Jesus deals."[3]

The family held in high esteem.—Turning now
to the indirect evidence of other teachings, we find
that Jesus holds the family in such high esteem that
he continually uses it as the type of the Kingdom.
While he often speaks of the kingdom of heaven,
he does not, in general, use the Kingdom imagery
which prevails in the Old Testament. But the
family words "father," "brother," "sons" are often
on his lips. No other words of human relationships
so well express those which should exist between
all men and between them and God. Try to
substitute "boss," "hands," "superintendent,"
"teacher," "pupil," "governor," "subject," or

[3] Peabody, *Jesus Christ and the Social Question*, p. 154.

"slave," and see how inadequate· they are. Divine love is understandable when pictured as paternal. Repentance is illustrated by the prodigal son when he exclaims, "I will arise and go to my father." "Repentance, that is to say, is but the homesickness of the soul." Jesus added brotherhood to the vocabulary of religion, and in trying to bring heavenly relationships within the comprehension of humans he could find no analogy better than the family.

However, Jesus' idea of the family reaches even a higher level—that of a divinely appointed institution. "What God hath joined together, let not man put asunder." This is not saying that all marriages are made in heaven—though they ought to be. It is, rather, to show that the institution has the approval of God. These high ideals are surely needed to-day. Their widespread adoption would dispel the selfishness and sordidness of matches made for money or social position. Such ideals would check hasty and ill-considered marriages. We joke about Gretna Green and Reno, "married in haste and repenting at leisure," soul affinities, and all the rest. Sincere love for our country and religious zeal alike would bid us rather to weep as we regard the implied menace to home life. To follow the Master's thought would lift the relationship of the sexes out of the realm of idle jesting and worse. Colored supplements (misnamed comic) that hold up discord and strife as the usual order of married life would fill us with disgust rather than merriment.

It may be necessary to recall that these ideals are for members of the Kingdom, for those who are in accord with the mind of Christ. They certainly transcended the Mosaic law, and perhaps modern legislation cannot yet reach their high idealism. But for Christian people at least there can be no doubt about standards. Marriage is a permanent relation; where separation is unavoidable no remarriage is to be considered. It is more than a personal contract, more than a social incident, more even than a social institution. It is a divinely appointed relation and as such is to be sacredly guarded. This high conception is well expressed in the beautiful and ancient vows of the English Church liturgy: "To have and to hold from this day forward, for better for worse, for richer, for poorer, in sickness and in health, to love and to cherish, till death do us part, according to God's holy ordinance."

EXERCISES

1. What reason do you have to suppose that Jesus would oppose polygamy? Is it forbidden in the gospel? Is it contrary to the spirit of the gospel?
2. How is modern divorce contrary to Christ's teaching?
3. Why is divorce increasing? What will help most in checking it?
4. How should the establishment of a less individualistic social order affect divorce?
5. Give some evidences of democracy in the ordinary family. Some undemocratic things.
6. What ideals of Christ are generally maintained in American homes? Which are most frequently violated?

7. How has the entrance of women into industry affected the home?
8. What is meant by "the family is the social unit"?
9. Show that "table-talk" has an educational value.
10. How does poor housing affect the family?
11. Is there a Housing Commission in your city? If so, what are its duties?
12. The home, when existing in comparative isolation, had many functions which in the complex life of a modern city have been more or less socialized. Discuss the means and extent of this socialization in each of the following:
    (a) Production of crops, food stuffs, and textiles.
    (b) Trade and barter.
    (c) Protection against marauding forces.
    (d) Protection against fire.
    (e) Prevention and cure of disease.
    (f) Education. General, technical, cultural.
    (g) Religious training.
13. Apply the four tests of Chapter VIII to the family. Is it Christian?

TOPICS FOR FURTHER STUDY

1. The historical forms of the family.
2. A study of the causes of divorce.
3. The family as a type of the kingdom of heaven.
4. The factory and the home.
5. Ancestor worship and the family.
6. The place of the family under socialism.
7. The ancient Hebrew patronymic family.
8. Relation of domestic science to family ideals.
9. Family life in the slums.

SUGGESTED READINGS

Adler, F., *Marriage and Divorce*.

Cope, H. F., *Religious Education in the Family*.

Mathews, *The Social Gospel*, Chapters IV, V, VI, XIII.

Peabody, *Jesus Christ and the Social Question*, Chapter III.

Rauschenbusch, *Christianizing the Social Order*, pp. 128–136, 262–271, 302–303.

Small and Vincent, *An Introduction to the Study of Society*, Book II, Chapters I to IV, and Book IV, Chapters II and III.

CHAPTER IX

THE SCHOOL

THE past two hundred years have witnessed the gradual democratization of the school in America. Sir William Berkely, governor of Virginia in 1670, piously thanked God that "we have no free schools." But the very thing that he feared has come to pass and is regarded as one of the proudest achievements of our national life. Education has become, in theory at least, the heritage of all. There may be an aristocracy of learning, but entrance to it is denied to none because of the accident of birth. This democratizing of education, this offering of its privileges to the humblest, not only upsets old ideas of caste, but constitutes a real step toward Christian ideals.

This transformation has also affected the curriculum of the school. The marked trend from the academic toward the practical is in answer to the demand that education must meet the needs of everyday life. It must be granted that mistakes have been made in the readjustments. All too often the school, in its anxiety to teach folk how to earn a living, has forgotten to instruct them in that vastly more important thing, how to live. Sometimes the attempt to make education practical has resulted in its becoming materialistic. We may, however, have faith in the outcome; idealism will have its counteracting influence and education will more and more nearly realize its ideal of enabling the child to function in all directions in its environment. There is still another indication of this change which has taken place since the Cavaliers of England and America regarded education as "a prerequisite of the secular and religious aristocracy." It is in the wider social use being made of the school plants. Parent-Teacher Associations meet at the schoolhouse. Lectures, special classes, discussion forums, and mothers' clubs enlarge the circle of its influence. Evening classes are provided for various groups not reached by the regular day sessions. In many neighborhoods the schoolhouse is a true social center. A similar extension is taking place in the institutions of higher learning. Colleges and universities are recognizing a responsibility for service to their communities. Able assistance is given in such fields as economics, civics, social service, engineering, business administration, medical and dental clinics, music, art, etc. This service is rendered through conferences, extension classes, lectures, membership on civic boards and other direct means.

The school and the church.—Historically there has been a very close connection between the school and the church. The catechetical and catechumenal schools conducted by the church during the early centuries of the Christian era led in time to the monastic school and later to the universities. During this time education was a definite part of the church's program. The teachers were clergy and the schools were attached to the monasteries and other church properties. Moreover, the curricula were strongly colored by ecclesiastical considerations. With the Revival of Learning came an increasing secularization of education. But even then the church maintained a lively interest, and particularly through the establishment and endowment of colleges has played an important part up to the very present. This has been especially true in America. In those early days of colonization, and later on the westward moving frontier, the churches were always the friends of education. They built academies and founded colleges, and out of their scanty resources raised endowments. "That enthusiasm for education, which is one of the finest characteristics of our country and has gone far to redeem us from the charge of mammonism, was kindled and fed by the churches and ministers, by the denominational academies and colleges, and by the men and women who were bred in them."

Thus there have been gradually laid aside certain old and unchristian ideals and customs. Class privilege in education has all but disappeared in educational circles. Private exploitation of the schools for financial gain has never been an outstanding evil and is a diminishing one surely. Service is more and more the watchword of the schools, and service is a thoroughly Christian idea. It is no mere chance that on the frontiers of civilization the school and the chapel stand side by side, indeed, often are housed in the same building. The church has been the patron of education; she has founded academies and colleges; the financial resources have been supplied by her members, and her young people have filled its classrooms. So it is by no means strange that essential Christian ideals should largely control in education.

The failure in religious training.—There is, however, an important side of human development which has been almost entirely untouched by the organized forces of education. It is in striking contradiction to the generally recognized modern educational principle that "the whole child goes to school." This is the vital point of moral and religious training, of spiritual development. Here the average school man has "virtually confessed himself helpless, a victim of baffled thought. . . . Meanwhile, who can aver that 'the whole child goes to school' when the child is the innocent victim of a system of schooling that assiduously excludes the special factor that makes for the unfolding of the spiritual nature? . . . Spiritual existence is the essential meaning of human life. Because the object of life is growth, because the ground of his culture lies in his own nature, because he possesses the divine powers of the soul, man is a greater name than prince or king! I believe a future generation of educational leaders will view with amazement the dullness and slowness of heart exhibited by our generation in stolidly blinking this fundamental issue."[1]

It is amazing that we can have been so shortsighted. The very success of our splendid American school system is in danger of becoming a menace, for it is a daring and dangerous thing to train a generation mentally and neglect them morally and religiously. An educated rascal is dangerous to the community in proportion to his keenness and training. A dishonest dullard soon bungles in his

---

[1] Hunt, "The New Education," Western Journal of Education, June, 1916.

petty crime and is discovered and punished. But couple low and immoral purposes to a trained mind, stored with knowledge, and a menacing personality is produced which may cause untold havoc in the social fabric. The crimes of such a one may reach appalling heights. Even more serious is the fact that he may keep inside the bounds of law and for a time at least win popular approval for his shrewdness. The plain fact is that while we have developed such an admirable system of secular education we have been exceedingly slack in provision for moral and religious training. People who would regard illiteracy as an intolerable disgrace view complacently the spiritual ignorance of their children. Communities spend thousands of dollars in splendid equipments for secular education, but make no provision for religious training other than the meager "penny" programs of the Sunday schools. These latter at their best leave large sections of the community unreached. Consider, for example, the relative time devoted to religious and secular training. The usual school day is five hours, which means one thousand hours per year of forty weeks. At the best a child receives in Sunday school fifty-two periods of from a half to three-quarters of an hour of religious training. This is further reduced by absences and various interruptions, so that it is doubtful if for the average child there is more than twenty-five hours of religious instruction annually.

A recent survey of a certain city revealed that over eight thousand boys and girls of school age were receiving no regular religious instruction of any kind. These constituted sixty-two per cent of the entire population within the school-age limits. The city is well churched, four of the leading churches having at the time the survey was made well developed plans of religious education under competent paid directors. It is a place of more than average wealth, culture, and religious vision. Whether religious training will be undertaken by the public school may be still an open question, though the preponderance of opinion is now against it. The tradition of the separation of Church and State lies at the foundation of this feeling, and is too essential an American doctrine to be easily set aside. Indeed, it must not be set aside, although there certainly is a reasonable doubt whether public instruction in morality and essential religion would constitute an infringement of this ancient and honored principle. This much is certainly clear, that some adequate program of religious instruction must be adopted. It is entirely probable that it will be conducted by the churches, but that it will be much more comprehensive than the present Sunday-school work. There must be an extension so as to include week-day instruction, and some satisfactory means of correlation with the system of secular education must be developed.

The last two decades have seen a growing appreciation of the need of better religious training. Great improvement has taken place in the curriculum material; some advance has been made in teacher training; higher standards in methods and equipment have been reached. The most important development now taking place in religious education is found in the movement for week-day religious instruction. It includes the Daily Vacation Bible

Schools, Accredited Bible Study, and plans for
week-day instruction in religion by the churches.
The training of teachers and leaders and the preparation of curriculum material are vital phases of
this work. The interest of public school men and
their sincere efforts to fit such instruction with the
child's weekly program are significant.

Making education Christian.—What are the Christian standards for education? We shall look in
vain for any dierct answer to this question in the
gospel. Certain standards may readily be deduced,
however, to which the school must conform if it
is to maintain its place in the Kingdom plans.
One of these has been referred to already. Nothing
could be more thoroughly unchristian than the
old idea of restricting education to a small "upper"
class. Instead of being an instrument of service
it was used as a badge of superiority, a means of
widening an unrighteous gulf. It is certainly the
desire of Christ that all his brethren should have
every chance for betterment and growth. It is
significant that every far-sighted missionary
endeavor has at some point included instruction.
A century ago zealous Catholic priests were establishing the chain of missions along the Camino
Real in California. These outposts of civilization
were centers of practical education as well as of
religious instruction. From the first, teaching and
evangelism have occupied places side by side in
the work among the Indians, and that plan is followed now by workers of all denominations. Foreign
missionaries have learned, sometimes after bitter
experience, that the teacher must ground well the
faith awakened by the preacher. Wherever the

spirit of Christ has had full sway men have been anxious to share their best with all their brothers.

Another unchristian tendency with which education has had to contend is its prostitution to selfish ends. Mr. Squeers, of Dotheboys Hall, may not exist to-day, but his selfish ignorance may still sometimes be found. The woman with little preparation and meager native teaching ability, who teaches to earn pin money; the man who finds fair pay and long vacations and a certain standing in the community a sufficient reward for his humdrum service, untouched by the sacred fire of the genuine teacher; the medical school or dental college run for revenue only—all these have felt the blighting touch of commercialism.

A fine thing about the school-room is that comparatively it is free to minister to the highest needs of the developing life. A ready and real test of its work is in its product. If the youth of our nation are showing a spirit of service, embodying the highest ideals of character under the acid test of practical living, growing out of selfishness into altruism, learning the lessons of race experience and expressing them in terms of social life, reaching out from the finite to the infinite, then the school is Christian.

EXERCISES

1. Does the grade school foster real social feeling?
2. Are colleges democratic?
3. In what grade do children begin to draw the color line and make class distinctions?
4. What high-school study broadened most your social outlook? How much did your age have

to do with this result? The teacher? The rest of the class?

5. Think of the relative value of various studies.
   (a) Arrange the following subjects in the order of their *practical* value: English, Grammar, Latin, geometry, physics, chemistry, history, Spanish, bookkeeping, arithmetic, English literature, physiology, geography.
   (b) Arrange the same list in the order of their value in developing the mental powers of the individual.
   (c) Arrange the same list in the order of their value in producing social outlook.

6. Should religion be taught in the public schools?

7. The ratio of time spent per year in Sunday school and day school is at best one to twenty. Is that enough? How can it be increased?

8. Should religious education be under the direction of the local church or should it be a community undertaking?

9. Give examples of the use of school equipment for community betterment, aside from instruction.

10. Describe some activities of Parent-Teacher Associations.

11. Whom does the P. T. A. help most—parents, teachers, or pupils?

12. When is education practical?

13. What should a trade school teach?

14. List the general subjects you would include in a college course in engineering, theology, education.

Topics for Further Study

1. The Gary educational plan.
2. The study of the Bible in the public school.
3. The function of the Christian college.
4. The origin of some American university.
5. Social studies in the grades.
6. "Cash value" as an element in education.
7. College graduates as social leaders.

Suggested Readings

Addams, *Democracy and Social Ethics*, Chapter VI.

Bogardus, *Introduction to Sociology*, Chapter XI.

Rauschenbusch, *Christianizing the Social Order*, pp. 142–147, 452–453.

Athearn, *Religious Education and American Democracy*, Chapter I.

CHAPTER X

THE STATE

A NATION must have territory, population, and a form of government. These characteristics distinguish it from those antecedent forms, the gens, the patriarchal family, and the tribe. Among primitive peoples crude governments were developed under the urge of fear and for the sake of mutual protection against common danger. Whether the danger was from their own kind or from wild animals, it was a bond of union and a potent force in developing leaders. This contest for power between the governing group and other social groups furnishes many an interesting historical chapter. Under a democracy society makes the government, and certain voluntary organizations may well exist and function socially with little or no relation to government. On the other hand, in an absolute monarchy government creates society and its very existence is conditional on control of the voluntary associations. The essential difference is indicated by Stukenburg when he says: "Its (the government) sphere is that of collective authority and coercion; the sphere of other societies is that of cooperation." Thus it transpires that socially our interest is in the third of the characteristics of the nation. If the state is an organism having functions and responsibilities, then government is its means of expression.

It is interesting that the classification of governments as monarchies, oligarchies, and democracies, made by Aristotle, anticipated the developments of many centuries. This classification indicates the place where the authority of government rests, and with this authority goes also obligation. Doctor McDonald said: "Democracy means the kingship of the common people. But kingship is not wearing robes of purple and crowns of gold. Kingship is bearing burdens and facing obligations and doing duties and rendering services. When the power of the king passed over to the crowd there passed with it that awful and inescapable obligation, the facing of which made the king either martyr or despot under the old regime, and under the new regime runs the risk of making the crowd either coward or criminal." It is this "inescapable obligation" which makes it necessary for citizens of the democracy to understand the source and expression of the authority of government.

The functions of the state.—This power and obligation of government may be defined by noting the functions of the state. They have sometimes been conveniently classified as constituent and ministrant. To the former belong such activities as the defense of the realm, preservation of the public order, coinage of money, enforcement of health laws, etc. Ministrant functions include postal service, education, control of industry, and many other things which conceivably could be carried on by private interests. In the past century the ministrant functions of government have been largely extended. In fact, much of the political discussion and difference of opinion of the day centers on the possible or advisable extension of these governmental activities.

Another classification, suggested by Doctor Bogardus, is threefold: (1) Activity with reference to other states, guaranteeing protection from external attack or undue interference; (2) activity with reference to its citizens, guaranteeing them security and liberty; (3) activity in promoting constructive measures for group advance.[1] As an immediate consequence of the first of these activities, the defense of the realm, sovereign states are frequently engaged in war. Some of these historical struggles have probably been necessary, and have made a certain contribution to human progress. Many have been utterly unjustifiable and wrong. Krehbiel, in his careful study, cites six arguments which have been advanced for war. These are:

1. War is inevitable.

   (a) It is a divine institution. "I believe war is the divinely appointed means by which the environment may be adjusted" (Maude, in *War and the World's Life*).

   (b) History confirms its inevitability. In the 3,357 years of known history prior to 1861 there were 3,130 years of war and 227 of peace.

   (c) Human nature, unchangeable, makes war inevitable. "Between states the only check on injustice is force" (Bernhardi).

---

[1] *Introduction to Sociology*, p. 188.

2. War exerts a wholesome moral influence.
   (a) Develops patriotism, unselfishness, efficiency, economy, inventiveness, cour-
   age, sense of social equality.
   (b) Preserves physical virility.
   (c) Aids progress by settling differences.
3. War performs the biological function of select-
   ing the best nation. Prevents overpopula-
   tion. Develops the race at expense of
   individual.
4. The economic advantage to the victor. Gain
   of territory or indemnity. Crushing competition.
5. The economic value of giving employment,
   teaching trades, etc., in the army.
6. Armies are useful in time of peace.

A detailed consideration cannot be attempted here.
As a national policy war is open to at least these
two serious objections: First, it rests on the fallacy
that might makes right. At the best, force only
hastens inevitable results. At its worst it only
retards them. Second, the economic folly of war.
As Norman Angell has so consistently pointed out,
the victor is by no means always the gainer.

Is war Christian? Here again we have no direct
gospel teaching. Indirectly Christ's high estimate
of individual worth, his emphasis on love as the
only successful life motive, his pleas for race solidarity, his exaltation of spiritual values are all
against it. Just as these principles become operative
in personal life will they become powerful in the
national life. "National morality cannot be far
in advance of individual morality." So it would
seem to be fundamental to any consideration of the

right or wrong of war that Christians should examine with frankness their acceptance of Jesus' message of love and brotherliness as the guiding principles in their personal relations. When they accept these and practice them so as to arrest the attention of the world, there will be some hope of winning the nations to the same program.

Law and punishment.—With reference to its internal affairs the function of government is exercised through legislation. Law is crystallized public opinion. As a constructive and corrective social force remedial legislation is the expression of what people think and desire, and when public opinion is not back of it law ceases to have power. Remedial legislation differs from criminal law in the objects of its enactments, which include such things as sanitation, fire hazard, sweat-shops, factory inspection, traffic regulation, hours of labor, etc. Not all evils can be cured by law, few can be cured without law. It forms one of the chief means for social control of individual conduct and relations. It follows that respect for law and order is one of the important props of civilization. Failure at this point is a sign of social disintegration. When, as often happens, a law no longer represents public opinion, it should be repealed, but not disregarded. The best way to get rid of a "dead-letter" law is to enforce it. Officers who attempt to discriminate and decide which laws "the people wish enforced" are going outside of their sphere. The peace officer's duty is to enforce laws as he finds them and not to attempt to interpret public opinion.

A government to be effective must be able to

enforce its will, that is, its laws. To this end punishment is necessary for those who transgress the laws and so record their lack of harmony with society and their disregard for social solidarity. The history of punishment is an interesting one. Originally, it was closely wrapped up with the idea of revenge on the part of the injured person or his friends. In time the criminal came to be regarded not only as the foe of the wronged individual, but the enemy of society as well, and punishment became a concern of the whole group. Even then retaliation long continued to be the underlying principle, and is not entirely eliminated even to-day. It is a deep-seated human instinct to want to get even and "an eye for an eye and a tooth for a tooth" makes a strong appeal. Early in the Middle Ages, under German influence, the idea of "compensation" arose as a substitute for or modification of revenge. By the payment of a sum of money, "*wergeld*," to the injured person, or later on to the state, almost any wrong—even murder—could be atoned for. Repression has been recognized as a basis for punishment. It is supposed to operate to prevent repetition of the crime and as a deterrent to others. This theory of suppression of crime has often led to horrible severity and tortures. There seems to be no doubt that the value of repression has been largely overestimated. It is the final argument for capital punishment. Revenge and repression must jointly bear the blame for the hideous history of inhuman methods of dealing with criminals.

Beccaria, an Italian writer, is credited with first effectively suggesting the idea of reformation in his little book on *Crimes and Punishment*, published in 1764. Others have contributed largely since then until it is a well-recognized principle to-day. Present-day thought includes three purposes of punishment: to provide a deterrent, to protect society by incarcerating those with criminal tendencies, and, finally, to reform the criminal. The spirit of Christianity has gradually permeated this department of public life. Such things as prison reform, probation, indeterminate sentences, compensation of prisoners for work done, graduation of penalty to suit crime, and juvenile courts are evidences of the effect of this spirit.

Some remnants of class distinction.—Some indication has been given throughout this chapter of Christian ideals as applied to the state. As to the form which government should take, essential democracy is indicated by the Christian principles of the value of personality and the solidarity of society. Where these hold sway there will not be much room for class distinction and special privilege. That special privilege is antagonistic to the spirit of Christ few would care to deny. The high places in the Kingdom are for those who stoop to lowly tasks of service. Not only is Christianity essentially democratic, but democracy is essentially Christian. While some rather long and rapid steps have been recently taken toward world democracy, special privilege—that most unchristian attribute of autocracy—dies hard. "Some remnants of this inequality still linger wherever feudal rank survives. A Russian noble and a moujik who commit the same offense do not receive the same punishment. . . . In Italy two cardinals recently claimed their right as Italian princes to have their deposition as witnesses taken in their own houses instead of coming into a public court like common people."[1] At least, however, in the United States, and increasingly in many other countries, the "denial of equal rights and of the equal humanity of all is felt to be a backsliding and a disgrace." The fight is not over and will not be as long as suspicion even remains that a poor man cannot get even-handed justice in any court, or while "the interests" can at all control elections or the course of legislation.

There might seem to be little call for discussion of the attitude of the Christian toward government. This would be true if there had not been some who seem to feel absolved from all political responsibilities by reason of their membership in the kingdom of heaven. They take very literally the injunction to come out and be separate from the world. They have somehow gained the idea that it is possible to live up to Jesus' measure of discipleship apart from human society. What the Christian attitude should be is indicated in the familiar saying, "Render therefore unto Cæsar the things which are Cæsar's; and unto God the things that are God's." Fortunately, we are not dependent on an isolated statement such as this. The whole trend of Jesus' teaching indicated acceptance of social responsibility and performance of social duties. Certainly, men have stood out against evil clothed in civic power, they have at times withstood magistrates vested with human authority which they were misusing. Such men have won the willing commendation of all who love human progress and human rights. It is surely of equal importance

[1] Rauschenbusch, *Christianizing the Social Order*, p. 149.

to maintain law when it is on the side of progress and right.

Exercises

1. Give an example of a special privilege in modern life.
2. What inequalities of privilege are recognized in the original Constitution of the United States?
3. Answer the arguments for war, namely:
   - (a) It is inevitable.
   - (b) It exerts a wholesome moral influence.
   - (c) It selects the best nation.
   - (d) Gives economic advantage to the victors.
   - (e) Provides employment and teaches trades.
   - (f) Armies are useful in time of peace.
4. Is it ever right for a nation to begin war?
5. Should a nation defend itself against wars of aggression?
6. "Is there any ideal of heroism that can take the place of those furnished by war?"
7. What should be the attitude of a Christian toward voting, office-holding, law-keeping?
8. Explain: "The best citizen of the commonwealth is he who gives fullest allegiance to the King of kings."
9. Should the church take sides, as an organization, in political issues?
10. Give example of the wholesome influence of the church on political life.
11. "Should a statesman be judged by his loyalty to his district, to his country, or by his personal morals?"

12. Why did Daniel Webster say, "Whatever makes men good Christians makes them good citizens"?
13. Should a "dead-letter law" be enforced?
14. Do you favor capital punishment?

TOPICS FOR FURTHER STUDY

1. Special privilege in American legislation.
2. The poor man's chance in the courts.
3. A moral substitute for war.
4. The peace time services of the army.
5. The church and the spirit of democracy.
6. The history of suffrage limitation in the United States.

SUGGESTED READINGS

Krehbicl, *Nationalism, War and Society*, particularly Chapter XVI.
Maude, *War and the World's Life*.
Rauschenbusch, *Christianizing the Social Order*, pp. 147–155.
Bogardus, *Introduction to Sociology*, Chapter VIII.
Wines, *Punishment and Reformation* Chapters III and IV.

CHAPTER XI

THE SHOP AND THE MART

INDUSTRIAL life presents so many varied aspects that it is extremely difficult to form correct judgments concerning it. It includes simple manual labor, the work of the highly skilled artisan and intellectual effort of many degrees. Production in mine and factory and on farm or oil field demands the constant labor of multitudes. Distribution and wholesale and retail trade necessitate another army of operatives. Special problems arise, such as employment of women and children, industrial accidents and disease, hours of labor and the seven-day week, unemployment, seasonal vocations, strikes, labor unions, and many others. Thus men and women are thrust into a thousand and one relationships through which the multitudinous operations of industry are carried on. Some must employ and some must be employed. Some must plan and direct, while others carry out the plans. There will be inevitable misunderstanding and injustice, simply because these are humans with all the limitations which that implies. But, however inevitable much of this maladjustment may be, there are great collective inhumanities from which our social and industrial life should be freed. Admitting, that is, that perfect social behavior cannot be expected, we may—and must—press on toward some great improvements.

In this brief chapter it is obvious that no extended discussion can be attempted. By considering some of the outstanding problems, a cross
section of industrial conditions may be formed.
To this end a few salient facts will be presented.
These have been selected to bring into view some
of the most unchristian aspects, the places most
remote from Kingdom ideals. This presentation,
therefore, must not be construed as a general charge
against all business and all employed therein. It
is intended, rather, to point out some places which
demand immediate and drastic action.

Childhood toiling.—Greed, in cowardly fashion,
always attacks those least able to care for themselves, so it need occasion no surprise to find little
children, women, and illiterate foreigners the vic-
tims of exploitation. Child labor is found in many
trades and occupations, the main ones being, according to the United States census, cotton manufacture, silk manufacture, glass manufacture, mining,
agriculture, fruit, vegetable and sea food canneries,
sweated clothing trades and street trades. The
census shows Texas to stand first in the number of
children ten to fifteen years old employed in gainful occupations. The figures for 1910 are as follows:

Texas,	114,000 boys	60,000 girls
Georgia,	102,000 boys	60,000 girls
Alabama,	94,000 boys	61,000 girls
North Carolina,	92,000 boys	53,000 girls
Mississippi,	83,000 boys	55,000 girls
South Carolina,	66,000 boys	52,000 girls
Pennsylvania,	64,000 boys	33,000 girls

All other States show lower figures.
The detrimental effects of child labor are many

and serious. (1) Physical. Growth and development are stunted when long hours are spent at tasks too heavy for the child's strength. One-sided development is frequent. Unsanitary conditions and lack of sufficient nourishing food are additional factors. (2) Educational. School days are shortened and sometimes cut off altogether, thus depriving the child of the much-needed training. Work after school hours tends to lessen mental activity and distract interest, thus lowering the efficiency of what instruction is received. (3) Moral. Government reports on women and child wage-earners indicate a tendency toward greater delinquency among working children.

The burden of responsibility for the existence of child labor must be shared by several classes. Actual economic need lies back of something less than one third of the cases, according to a Federal Report.[1] Sickness, death of a parent, etc., are

CAUSES OF CHILD LABOR

Economic necessity.. 30   per cent
Help desired, but not needed........27.9 per cent
Dissatisfaction with school.... ......26.6 per cent
Child prefers to work............... 9.8 per cent
Other causes.... .... 5.7 per cent

contributing causes which bring many families to the point of partial dependence on childish earning capacity. Then there is the greed of parents, for the same report finds "help desired, but not necessary," in almost another third. "Many parents, especially some immigrant parents, still consider their growing children as capital or economic assets from which financial returns in the form of

[1] *Federal Report on Women and Child Wage-Earners*, vol. vii, p. 46.

wages may be immediately received."[2]   Much of
the responsibility for child labor must be laid at
the door of the employer. He often willingly accepts
the underpaid services of children. Nearly every
attempt to secure child labor legislation has had
its shameful chapter of opposition from the employers
in affected industries. Again, the public, in its
indifference and ignorance of the baleful results,
must accept a large share of the blame.

A hopeful sign is found in the increasing amount
of legislation. A very helpful agency has been the
National Child Labor Committee, which has supplied information, stimulated public interest, and
agitated for legislation. The laws are in the main
State laws providing for minimum age limits, educational qualifications, prohibition of night work,
and protection from dangerous trades. While the
provisions of these laws vary in different States,
they usually establish the minimum age for full-
time work at from fourteen to sixteen years, provide
for schooling at least through the grammar grades,
specify certain prohibited industries, and otherwise
guard the welfare of the adolescent worker.

Women in industry.—More than eight million
women and girls were employed in gainful occupations in 1910 in the United States. That is to
say, about one quarter of all the women over ten
years of age in the country. New York led in
numbers, with 984,000. The proportion of women
and girls so employed in the United States is steadily
increasing, and has been rapidly growing for a
number of years. Some of the more serious results
may be noted.

---

[2] Bogardus, *Introduction to Sociology*, p. 158.

1. It frequently means neglect of the home. In 1916 it was estimated that nearly one million married women were employed. In many cases this involves neglect of young children. The withdrawal of the mother or wife usually results in a lower standard home.

2. Wages are affected. Women are commonly paid less than men and frequently replace them. In many industries women and men are employed under the same conditions as to work done and hours kept. It is unusual, however, for women to receive the same wage. The average wage for women in 1900 was only a little over half that paid to men. This is due in part to the rapid increase of women employed in industry, thus creating a supply much in excess of the demand. Then, too, a large proportion of these women are unskilled laborers who receive correspondingly low wages.

3. Detrimental moral and physical effects often result. Women undertake work unsuited to their strength. Long hours, involving continuous standing, constant mental tension, unsanitary surroundings, are some of the elements involved.

In seeking for the causes underlying this startling increase in the employment of women, two reasons stand out prominently. The first of these is the introduction of labor-saving machinery. These tools have increased production and relieved men of the heavy tasks of hand production. The lighter work of attending these automatic or semi-automatic machines can be done at least as well by women, and in many cases their superior dexterity enables them to excel men. Thus we find thousands of women operatives in cotton mills, workers in electric manufactories, and in binderies, etc. Another important consideration is the constantly increasing cost of living, coupled with the relatively low wage paid many men. In every recent census the average yearly wage earned by men has been considerably under the most conservative estimate of the necessary family income. This means either substandard living conditions for the family, or the necessity of augmenting its income by the labor of women and children.

Some legislation has been passed relative to the employment of women. These laws, in general, establish an eight-hour day, set minimum wages, and limit employment to certain industries. The largest hope for improvement lies in public education and the development of a social conscience. If the untoward effects on the home and the younger generation can be widely realized, one step at least has been taken toward correction.

Maimed and helpless workers.—The grim toll of industrial accidents and occupational diseases is not commonly appreciated. The casualties of the World War were numbered in millions, but the losses of peace are not less appalling. Ten years ago one in every 181 of the population was killed or wounded in an industrial accident each year. The railroads are responsible for a large number of these. In 1907 the report of the Interstate Commerce Commission recorded 5,000 killed and 76,286 injured. The figures of the last decade, when available, will not probably show any marked change. The appalling thing is the frequent indifference to human life in comparison with financial loss. Profits have nearly always been put ahead of human life.

"The miners say if a mule is killed in the mines, the superintendent wants to know how it happened; if a man is killed, they take him out of a side door." Manufacturing processes, like some used in the making of sulphur matches, which result in horrible occupational disease, are continued because the safer substitute involves a higher cost. The use of automatic couplers by the railway companies reduced the number of accidents enormously, but their adoption was stoutly opposed by the managers.

Another dark corner of modern industry is the tenement labor. Usually not coming under the supervision of factory inspection departments, long hours and poor pay are the rule. It is in such surroundings that the "sweatshop" flourishes. "Technically, a sweatshop is a tenement house kitchen or bedroom, in which the head of the family employs outside persons not members of his immediate family, in the manufacture of garments for some wholesale merchant tailor." The term has been extended to include other industries, such as the making of other clothing, feathers, fur, and artificial flowers. It is also often applied to any factory, laundry, or shop where hours are long, pay inadequate, and surroundings unhealthful. Usually the industry is one requiring little or no machinery, where piece work may be done by a low-grade type of labor. The work is frequently taken home. An investigation in New York of 204 homes where such work was carried on brought to light some of the prices paid. For example, finishing coats, 6 cents each; making babies booties, 25 cents per dozen. Such workers could earn from $2.50 to

$3.50 per week. A family consisting of a mother and two children made feather plumes. Working for a day and a third, they tied 8,613 knots in *one* plume and earned $2.10, which is at the rate of one cent for each 41 knots. In this same investigation, it was found that 25 per cent of the workers were under 10 years of age; 45 per cent were under 14, and 60 per cent under 16 years. Three quarters of these families earned less than 10 cents per hour as the total wage of the whole group.

It is, of course, to be expected that bad housing conditions result: families of four or five, with perhaps a boarder, living in a single room. Contagious diseases spread with rapidity, and the whole moral and sanitary tone is so low as to constitute a social menace.

The idolatry of mammonism.—These snapshots at some of the dark shadows of the industrial world may serve to suggest the sources of its social blackness. Reduced to its simplest term, there is no better statement than six words spoken by Jesus: "Ye cannot serve God and mammon." The taproot of business is profit, and competition is the modern business way of making profits.

"Thus our capitalistic commerce and industry lies alongside of the home, the school, the church, and the democratized state as an unregenerate part of the social order, not based on freedom, love, and mutual service, as they are, but on autocracy, antagonism of interests, and exploitation. Such a verdict does not condemn the moral character of the men in business. On the contrary, it gives a remarkable value to every virtue they exhibit in business, for every act of honesty, justice, and kindness is a triumph over hostile conditions, a refusal of Christianity and humanity to be chilled by low temperature or scorched by the flame of high pressure temptation. . . . Life is holy. Respect for life is Christian. Business, setting profit first, has recklessly used up the life of the workers. . . . Beauty is a manifestation of God. Capitalism is ruthless of the beauty of nature if its sacrifice increases profit. . . . These are the points in the Christian indictment of capitalism. All these are summed up in this single challenge, that capitalism has generated a spirit of its own which is antagonistic to the spirit of Christianity; a spirit of hardness and cruelty that neutralizes the Christian spirit of love; a spirit that sets material goods above spiritual possessions. To set Things above Men is the really dangerous practical materialism. To set Mammon before God is the only idolatry against which Jesus warned us."[1]

One need not share Professor Rauschenbusch's conviction that socialism is the remedy for these conditions to agree with his arraignment of greed and selfishness. The debasement of the individual and the shattering of brotherhood were abhorrent to Jesus. His kingdom is still far off while men strive in selfish forgetfulness and put the things of sense above those of spirit.

"As He went out to resume His Journey, there came a man running up to Him, who knelt at His feet and asked,

" 'Good Rabbi, what am I to do in order to inherit the Life of the Ages?' . . .

---

[1] Rauschenbusch, *Christianizing the Social Order*, pp. 313–315.

"Then Jesus looked at him and loved him, and said,

" 'One thing is lacking in you: go, sell all you possess and give the proceeds to the poor, and you shall have riches in Heaven; and come and be a follower of mine.'

"At these words his brow darkened, and he went away sad; for he was possessed of great wealth.

"Then looking around on His disciples, Jesus said,

" 'With how hard a struggle will the possessors of riches enter the Kingdom of God!'

"The disciples were amazed at His words. Jesus, however, said again,

" 'Children, how hard a struggle is it for those who trust in riches to enter the Kingdom of God! It is easier for a camel to go through the eye of a needle than for a rich man to enter the Kingdom of God.' "[2]

EXERCISES

1. Name the most serious industrial problem in your city.
2. What is the age limit for child labor in your State?
3. Give first-hand impressions of child labor. Of women in industry.
4. What is a sweatshop? What industries are carried on in them?
5. Give some causes for child labor.
6. Why is the accident rate for children in industry higher than for adults?
7. Give arguments for and against a minimum wage.

[2] Mark 10: 17–25, Weymouth Version New Testament.

8. What is industrial insurance?
9. Can you find any warrant in the gospel for objecting to (*a*) child labor, (*b*) a twelve-hour day, (*c*) use of unguarded machinery?
10. When is competition unchristian?
11. Explain: "Whenever life is set above profit in business, there is a thrill of admiration which indicates that something unusual has been done."
12. Is our economic system a friend to beauty?
13. Would it be easier to live a Christian life under socialism than under capitalism?
14. Which is worse, a twelve-hour day and a six-day week, or an eight-hour day and a seven-day week?

Topics for Further Study

1. The federal child-labor law.
2. Children and the sea-food industries.
3. Industrial insurance in the United States.
4. Minimum-wage legislation.
5. Sweated industries.
6. Christ's attitude toward wealth.
7. Influence of industry on the church.

Suggested Readings

Bulletins of the National Child Labor Committee.
Rauschenbusch, *Christianizing the Social Order*, Part 3, Chapters III–VII; Part 4, Chapters I–VII.
Christianity and the Social Crisis, pp. 276–279.
Stelzle, *American Social and Religious Conditions*, Chapter IV.
Ward, *The Social Creed of the Churches*, particularly Chapters II, III, IV, and IX.

CHAPTER XII

PLAY

PLAY has emerged from a place of neglect, or even repression, to one of importance as a social factor. This change has been marked by several new attitudes. Time was when play was thought of as a relatively harmless, but useless, juvenile activity. It served to occupy children who were too young for anything useful. So it was held by some that play was the expression of the surplus energy of the child. Another explanation offered was the so-called recapitulation theory which supposed that in his play the child was repeating the history of the race in its past stages. Thus he passes through the various phases of savagery and barbarism, and later reaches in team plays the cooperation of civilization. This is really but a special application of the general theory of the child's development, which, while having some merit, may easily be pressed too far.

More recently play is being defined as a preparation for life. Muscles are strengthened, nerves trained, and coordination of action developed. "In playing with a spool, that is, in rolling and catching a spool, a kitten is getting ready for catching mice. The kitten is thereby developing claw and eye coordination that in a short time will be necessary for procuring food." In a similar way the doll plays of the girl prepare for motherhood, and the more active plays of the small boy look forward to the strenuous business of the workaday world. It naturally follows that play is becoming recognized as an important factor in education. "It is not something that a child likes to have; it is something that he must have if he is ever to grow up." Training through play has social as well as individual values. Through it the growing child learns how to live with others, discovers the value of cooperation, and gains respect for law through regard for the rules of the game. It is true, indeed, that the battles of England have been won on the playgrounds of her schools.

New attitudes toward play.—A new relation has been established between play and education. "All work and no play makes Jack a dull boy," was an accurate representation of the schoolmaster's opinion. Play was valuable only as a relaxation from the serious work of education. Froebel and Pestalozzi and Gross have helped us to realize that play is an integral and vital part of the educational process. From kindergarten to university recreation has been made part of the program. Not only, then, has the value of play in the development of childhood been established, but it is discovered to be more than a juvenile activity. The way in which the adult works, depends much on how he plays. "Civilization," says Frederic C. Howe, "depends largely on the way the people use their leisure," and Percy MacKaye, in the Civic Theater, says that the use of a nation's leisure is a test of its civilization. Recreation becomes, therefore, a matter of community interest. It is an important life function at all ages.

An important factor in this new attitude toward adult recreation is found in the changed conditions of labor. Our grandfathers divided their day into two parts—twelve hours of labor and twelve hours at home. To-day there are three periods of eight hours each, one for work, one for sleep, and the third for leisure. But this change, due to the shortened day, is not the only one which changed methods in industry have produced. The old-fashioned homes, with their yards and porches, have given way to flats and apartments. With the passing of the old-fashioned home have gone also the old-fashioned pleasures. The increased leisure is not spent in the home, but on the streets, in the city parks, and at various public amusements. Then, too, there is to be considered the effect of our modren high-pressure industrial life. Men as well as machines are speeded up under the demands of increased production. This strain upon the nerves of working people has resulted in an increased need for recreation. The permanent place of recreation in industry is further evidenced by the widespread vacation habit. A period of from one week to a month, frequently with pay, is regarded as part of the normal arrangement in many occupations. The week-end or Sunday trip to beach, mountain, or lakeside is also a fixture in many lives.

Another interesting evidence of a changed estimate of the value of play may be noted in criminology. As the idea of reformation has growingly controlled the methods of dealing with lawbreakers, recreation has found a place in the prison routine. Baseball grounds, moving pictures, and libraries have come to be part of the prison equipment. A needed extension of this principle is to many of the city and county jails. Persons, some of them innocent of any offense, but merely awaiting trial, are confined in these jails for periods from a few days to many months, and usually with no recreational facilities. The detrimental effect of such a period on the physical, mental, and moral well-being may easily be imagined.

Play and the church.—Perhaps nowhere has the new valuation of recreation as a vital life factor been more marked than in the church. The stern repression of colonial days has come down to us in a word, "puritanical," which often misleads us in our estimate of the sturdy virtues of those olden times. Puritan and Quaker alike, in turning against all too evident excesses and dangers of pleasure, missed also the value and need of real recreation. Some remnants of this attitude remain in repressive regulations to be found in certain communions. In general, however, the church is learning to use amusements rather than to try vainly to eliminate them. Modern religious education has a very definite place in its program for recreation and social life. Gymnasiums, playgrounds, boys and girls' clubs, inter-Sunday-school baseball leagues, social occasions, moving pictures, recreation camps, game rooms, lectures and concerts are among the recreational facilities of the church. This understanding attitude in relation to play is made clear by many writers on religious education. Professor George A. Coe says: "Just as the gap between the school and play is being filled up, so the home and church should now at last awake to the divine significance of the play instinct and make use of

it for the purpose of developing the spiritual nature.
The opposition between the play spirit and the
religious spirit is not real, but only fancied. . . .
We teach children to think of their most free and
spontaneous activities—their plays—as having no
affinity for religion, and then we wonder why religion does not seem more attractive to them as they
grow toward maturity!"[1]

Commercialized play.—The outstanding recreational problem is, of course, that of commercialized
amusements. "Pleasure resorts run for profit are
always edging toward the forbidden." A survey of
the places where commercial recreation is offered
in a single state[2] revealed thirty-four types, including theaters, pool rooms, ball parks, boat-houses,
dance halls, mountain resorts, etc. Under these
thirty-four heads were reported 9,826 places, including 4,596 saloons, the largest single item; 1,400
pool and billiard rooms; and others in varying
numbers down to nine riding academies. Sixteen
classifications, including about 7,800 of the individual amusement places, were of types involving
more or less definite moral hazard. Leaving out the
saloons, since eliminated entirely by the prohibition
act, this means that over one-half of these public
amusements were likely to be found "edging toward
the forbidden."

An investigation in New York city showed that
more than forty per cent of the pupils of the grade
schools learn to dance in the commercial dance
academy or public dance hall, and that a large

---

[1] Coe, *Education in Religion and Morals*, p. 144.
[2] *Report of the Recreational Inquiry Committee of the State of California.*

proportion of these young people continue to frequent these places. "In the better class dancing academies no liquor is sold, considerable supervision is exercised over the character of the persons allowed, and 'tough dancing' is prohibited. But in the academies of a lower type less supervision is exercised, and men and women of questionable character are present. . . . The dance hall is different in many ways from the dancing academy. It varies in nature from a great public place to 'the back room of the saloon, in which couples sit around at tables, and from time to time rise and whirl to the music of an unpleasant piano.' . . . The California Report states that of all recreations, public dance halls bear the most direct and immediate relation to the morals of their patrons. It is further known that this influence, as at present exerted, is extremely destructive."[1]

In visiting an amusement park such as is found at many seaside resorts, one is struck by the paucity of ideas for amusement. The changes are rung on a few well-worn types of entertainment. Games of chance, roller coasters, merry-go-rounds, crazy-houses, lunch counters, movie shows, and dancing pavilion nearly complete the list. Certainly, complete mental relaxation should be easily found. Rested nerves and moral tone are quite another matter, however. This suggests the distinction between amusement and recreation. Amusement is passive; it is the part of the spectator; it aims to divert, to while away the time, to provide change and excitement. Recreation is re-creation, its purpose is to renew strength, to refresh. It depends

[1] Bogardus, *Introduction to Sociology*, p. 121.

more on inward resource. The two are not mutually exclusive, neither does one necessarily include the other. There is no real recreation in many amusements. It is nothing less than tragic that so many folks seem so dependent on external sources of amusement, are so lacking in inner resources. It gives evidence of untrained and shallow souls.

Socialized play.—Over against the great mass of commercialized amusements may be placed an increasing number of socialized means for play. With the growing recognition of their social value has come an enlarging social conscience. One valuable social agency is the playground, which movement began to attain prominence about 1900. By 1913, 2,400 playgrounds had been established in 342 American cities, with more than 6,000 paid supervisors and workers. Some of the play problems are:

1. To keep a proper balance between the two parts of play, recreation and amusement.

2. To direct the children's play without loss of spontaneity.

3. To provide playgrounds and other uncommercial recreation facilities for all elements of the population.

4. To regulate commercialized amusements.

5. The development of home recreation so far as possible.

The socialization of the schoolhouse has been referred to in another chapter. Neighborhood Associations, Parent-Teacher Associations, and similar organizations are constantly growing in number and in the value of their community service. The Men's Clubs of some churches have cooperated.

Altogether hundreds of such social centers exist in schools, churches, women's club houses, social settlements, and even a few specially constructed buildings. Where these are used as recreation centers they are by no means confined to the lighter forms of play. Games, gymnastics, plays, and moving pictures are, of course, included. There are also to be found study classes, clubs for civic improvement and other means of providing recreation of a little different nature, but equally valuable.

Ward makes the following suggestions of activities in connection with the recreation center:

1. Its advantages should not be limited to the poorer section of the city.

2. Each school building used as a recreation center to have a large electric sign.

3. Glee clubs and choral societies should be organized under proper musical direction.

4. At least once or twice a week mothers' clubs should meet in the cooking-room of the school and very practical lessons in plain cooking and economic housekeeping be given.

5. Classes in simple sewing.

6. Nurses could give practical lessons.

7. Civil service classes for those wishing to join the fire and police forces should be organized.

He then adds, "Theodore Roosevelt recently said of the playgrounds: 'They are the greatest civic achievement the world has ever known.' Recreation centers are really the playgrounds of our adults. Effectively equipped and wisely directed, they can be made of the highest value in the conservation of the youth of our city, who are to be the citizens of the future and upon whose training and patriotism the welfare of our country depends."[1]

Pageantry has come to occupy an important place in community recreation. It stimulates a spirit of cooperation for the common welfare, frequently develops latent talent, and brings into pleasant and productive comradeship those who would otherwise not know each other. When the pageant deals with local history, as is often the case, a healthful community pride is developed. Three types of pageant have been evolved in America. First, the parade of emblematic floats and marching companies. Second, an out-of-doors performance. This is what is commonly understood by the term "pageant." It has been very extensively developed and presents an almost unlimited opportunity for action and spectacle. The third form is the indoor entertainment, which differs from the second only in limitations of space and setting. "The real pageant is given out of doors, its spectators number thousands, genuine distance gives its beauty to the production, the stage is as vast as the eye can reach, and the production aims to reproduce actuality rather than illusion."

The activities of the neighborhood center are found to include the following:

Civic activities. The public forum, new citizens receptions, public discussions and lecture.

Educational activities. Exhibition, lectures, art exhibits, classes.

Entertainment activities. Dramatics, moving pic-

---

[1] Ward, *The Social Center*, pp. 268, 270. D. Appleton & Company, publishers.

tures, singing, lectures, stunt night, dancing, community singing.

Recreational and physical activities. Gymnastics,
games, folk dancing, athletics, indoor games such as
chess and checkers, bowling.

Neighborhood service activities. Clinic for mothers
and babies, library and reading room, educational
guidance, handicraft instruction.

The church is also making its contribution toward
socialized recreation. The possibility of its doing
so is found in the changed attitude toward recreation
already referred to, and this in turn roots back
into the understanding that mirth and play are
not foreign to the spirit of Jesus. Still more than
that, they are coming to be recognized as essential
to a well-rounded Christian character. This means
that such play as contributes to truer manhood, to
healthier living and to better thinking is the right
and duty of every Christian. With the recognition
of this character building importance of recreation,
two changes have come in the attitude of the church.
One is the passing of many ancient restrictions, the
unfettering of the spirit of play. The other is the
definite inclusion of recreation as one field in which
the church should render its ministrations.

Constructively, the church is proceeding in accord
with this spirit of whole person living. It is recognizing the place of play in the program of religious
education and making use of these spontaneous
activities of childhood to enliven interest in instruction. It sees that it has a real duty to provide
wholesome amusement for its young people. It co-
operates with playgrounds and other community
enterprises.

Exercises

1. How do the amusements of to-day differ from those of our grandfathers?
2. Should moving pictures be censored?
3. What socialized amusements are there in your neighborhood?
4. What commercialized amusements are there in your neighborhood?
5. Has the spirit of play lessened the effectiveness of school discipline?
6. Why did the Puritans object to amusements?
7. Should the church legislate against specific amusements?
8. What recreation equipment would you provide in an ideal church building?
9. How does recreation differ from amusement?
10. What proportion of one's leisure should be given to recreation? to amusement?
11. How does the neglect of recreation warp one's development?
12. Do college athletics contribute helpfully to a student's life?
13. What is the greatest contribution of the moving picture? Its greatest drawback?
14. Has your community a recreation center? If so, what activities are carried on there?

Topics for Further Study

1. History of the playground movement.
2. Censorship of moving pictures.
3. Home recreation.
4. Inter-collegiate athletics.
5. The Boy Scout movement.
6. Pageantry and community play.

SUGGESTED READINGS

Bates and Orr, *Pageants and Pageantry*, Introduction. Meredith, *Pageantry and Dramatics in Religious Education*.

Bogardus, *Introduction to Sociology*, Chapter V.

California Report of the Recreational Inquiry Committee.

Community Recreation, published by the Playground and Recreation Association of America.

Ward, *The Social Center*, Chapters XII, XIII, XIV, and XV.

Whitaker, *The Gospel at Work in Modern Life*, Chapter XI.

Richardson, *The Church at Play.*

PART THREE

THE CHALLENGE TO THE CHURCH

The passing centuries have fronted the church with many problems. None of these situations have been more challenging than the present changing social order. How will the church meet this challenge which is also its chance? The answer to that question is of vast importance both to the social order and to the church. Intelligent, forward-looking leadership is imperative. Can and will the church supply that leadership? Mere good intentions will not suffice.

It will not be possible in these closing chapters to even outline a social program for the church, much less discuss it in detail. Certain directions of effort are, however, plainly indicated, and these may be suggested. Above all, the note of hope should be sounded. There are signs that constitute veritable "Channel Buoys of Progress."

CHAPTER XIII

A SPIRITUAL BASIS FOR SOCIAL IDEALS

When the Master said to Peter and Andrew, "Come ye after me and I will make you to become fishers of men," the record adds that *straightway* they left all and followed him. The promptness of their decision marks them as unusual men, for it is always hard to estimate correctly spiritual values. They decided promptly and correctly between the ideals proffered them by a wandering and obscure teacher and the easily appreciated worth of the good business which they so suddenly forsook. To give due weight to the intangible and unseen is never easy in the presence of the evident and material. The schoolboy who weighs the probable value of a college education against the present prospect of a job; the politician who hesitates between the vagueness of an approving conscience and the power and profits of an unrighteous course; the Christian who underestimates the power of prayer—each of these is encountering this problem.

Doubt of spiritual values.—The times in which we live have been more than doubtful of the value of the spiritual life. Of material prosperity there has been much, and men have been satisfied by it. They have had no unsatisfied soul-hunger. It is even more tragic that those who have lacked in abundance of possessions have supposed that to be their only lack. They too have had no soul-hunger. It is in such a spirit that much of the struggle for social justice has gone on. Too often injustice and wrong have bulked less large than the *results* of such attitudes. Here, again, it is the failure to estimate correctly the intangible and invisible values. It is not easy always to remember that hunger and squalor and ignorance, and even vice, are less serious than the unsocial and unchristian spirit which makes possible these conditions. When we do get the true perspective in these things, we will pity the man with the starved soul who is content to fatten his body on the rents of a tenement house even more than we will pity the tenant with the undernourished body.

Even if some social philosophy could be devised and put into operation which would remove all the inequalities and injustices and put the material world to rights, there would still be needed a return to spiritual life to save from barrenness. It is with these things in mind that we will proceed to consider some of the implications of a spiritual basis for social ideals.

A sound foundation needed.—*A spiritual basis is essential to successful social reform.* "A man is standing on the top of one of the giant 'skyscrapers' of New York viewing that great city. He turns to a companion and asks, 'If you wanted to make this city a city of God and establish the kingdom of God here, what would you do?'

"The companion answers, after a moment's thought: 'I would clean up those tenements; I would reduce street-car fares, to relieve that tenement congestion, and let those laborers live in the country. I would raise the wages of working girls. I would wipe out the vice districts, and drive out the grafting and corrupt politicians. I would Americanize those foreigners. I would prosecute every one who preyed upon the poor. I would tear down those Fifth Avenue palaces, open only a month or two in a year, and make playgrounds for the children. I would have cleaner streets and better sanitation. I would give every man a fair chance, and then I should have a city of God.'

"'I doubt it,' replies the first speaker, 'for if you didn't clean up the hearts of those people, you would probably have as much of hell as before, notwithstanding your improved conditions. Most of that suffering is caused by the sin and selfishness within men.'"[1]

This thought has already been emphasized in the chapters on "The Worth of a Man" and "A New Dynamic." Mere rearrangement of outer circumstances will not do. There must also be a cleaning up of the spirits of men. It takes sound individuals to build a sound social order.

Contentment rests not on things.—*Contentment needs a spiritual basis*. The inadequacy of the materialistic basis for contentment is everywhere evident. Those who have are just as unhappy, though from different causes, perhaps, as those that have not. All the philosophers have insisted that one's attitude toward life is the really important thing. There is a certain type of motor-minded man immersed in a sea of "practical" things who scoffs at the idealist. In the long run, however,

---

[1] Holmes, *Jesus and the Young Man of To-day*, pp. 13, 14.

idealism comes out ahead. Some one has said that there are two ways to be contented. One is to have what you want, the other is to want what you have. This does not indicate a spineless acceptance of circumstances, a mere clodlike attitude toward life. It is, rather, the spirit of Henry van Dyke's well-known words, "to be content with my possessions, but not satisfied with myself until I have made the most of them." Such a spiritual basis for contentment is in a measure independent of the lack of material comforts; it is even proof against their possession.

For the spiritual life, like the intellectual life and the cultural life, diverts attention and activity from primitive, antisocial interests to acquired interests that are socializing.

Our primitive, animal, untaught interests are interests of hunger and passion and of savage strife; and if we devote our attentions and activities to these, and these alone, we inevitably clash with one another, and social chaos must result. But, as Professor Ross wittily, though almost irreverently, says, the exerciser of dogs in training would be wise not to throw them a bone, but, rather, to set them baying the moon, for there might not be bone enough to go around, whereas there would be plenty of moon for all. So with the higher intellectual culture and spiritual interests of man. Attention and activity devoted to them seldom breed disagreements or generate friction. Just to the degree that we occupy ourselves with these higher interests, to that degree does social order develop. And of all these acquired socializing interests to which men may devote their attention, and from which they may secure happiness, the religious interests are most cheaply produced and distributed among the common people. It requires tremendous effort and capital to distribute widely all the products of science, philosophy, literature and art; but men pray instinctively, the religious life is spontaneous, and a revival can sweep through a whole population, redirecting the energies of the masses as nothing else can do."[1]

This is by no means an ascetic attempt to eliminate the physical from our scheme of living. It is, rather, an attempt to restore some higher values to their proper place, to suggest that living is fully as important as earning a living, that the power of spirit is great enough to bring joy and satisfaction and contentment in spite of any kind of circumstances. Yet, as we shall immediately consider, this does not imply at all satisfaction with circumstances that are wrong. It is a vastly different thing to be contented of mind in the midst of our environment, and to be contented with that environment. So, we move at once to the second implication, namely:

A reservoir of power.—*The spiritual life lays hold on power.* It is not a mere anodyne, something to keep the minds of people occupied so that they might forget their misery. If this were true, the strictures of some social leaders on religion and the church would be true. In fact, the Christian life not only furnishes high ideals and fine examples of living, it also supplies the needed dynamic.

This positive socializing power is manifested in the linking-up of religious life and emotions to social

[1] Finney, *Personal Religion and the Social Awakening*, p. 90.

ideals and activities. "Thus men are motivated to lives of spontaneous and positive goodness." Innumerable examples might be cited of the social power of religious idealism. Unfortunately, this power has been directed sometimes into fanatical and useless channels. It is hard, for example, to find warrant for the suffering and death of the little children led out of France and Germany in the Children's Crusades. But the power of ideals is undoubted, and may be harnessed to useful ends.

It is certainly no mere accident that the finest Christian idealism exists side by side with the highest social living. There is significance in the inextricable mingling of the Renaissance and the Reformation, in the religious fervor of many anti-slavery leaders, in the close cooperation of the church and the prohibition forces. The church has stood on all frontiers, intellectual as well as physical, of civilization; and by the same token the pioneer spirit that led men to dare the dangers of untrod paths around the world was often one with the spirit of missionary zeal. It will not do to forget that our forefathers planted the seeds of liberty in this land under the urge of religious idealism.

The doubt has been often expressed whether a zeal for the social interpretations of the gospel might not minimize the personal message. As some one put it, "Salvation, not soap and soup, is the concern of the church." Such a view indicates a wrong conception of the ends of personal salvation as well as of the fundamentals of social salvation. Men are not saved simply to free them from a just retribution. They are "saved to serve," and service according to the teaching of Jesus is defined in terms of neighborliness and "cups of cold water." On the other hand, as already indicated, no social reform can hope to succeed except as it lays hold on power through realized ideals. Is it not clear, then, that the hope of the world is in the ideals of Jesus—the finest ever set before humanity? "This is one of the lessons of the Cross: righteousness and love and the effort to give justice involve men in struggle and loss and suffering. Jesus did not call men to any easier life that he himself lived. Whoever followed him was to take up his cross and follow the Master as he carried his. And the same call comes to the Christians of to-day. True, we do not have to face the rack, and gallows, and the stake; but there are other things that a man must face who would attempt to put the principles of Jesus into social life. He must face misunderstanding, misrepresentation, envy, slander. Sometimes he must face financial loss, and even ruin, as well as loss of friendships. But the call to such heroic self-sacrifice is always to be heard. The disciple of the Son of man must, like his Master, seek to minister, not to be ministered unto. Thus only can he live out that real life which it is the mission of the gospel to beget within him."[1]

In the last analysis the program of the kingdom of God is one of social betterment, to be established by winning individuals to allegiance to Jesus Christ. Has ever a stronger evangelistic appeal been made? The call to interest in the social interpretation of the gospel is a call for personal consecration. It is a call for clean personal living. It is a call to

[1] Mathews, *The Social Gospel*, pp. 162, 163.

unfeigned acceptance of the mastery of the Christ in personal and social life.

EXERCISES

1. Give some evidences that the present age is "skeptical of spiritual life."
2. What ideals (not necessarily religious) are operating powerfully in America to-day?
3. What does Eucken mean by saying that we need more "depth of life"?
4. Name some great political movements undertaken under the urge of a great ideal. Some religious movements. Some social movements.
5. What is essential to contentment of mind?
6. Name some primitive instincts. Are they social or anti-social?
7. Name some acquired interests and contrast them with the primitive as to social qualities.
8. Name some of civilization's frontiers where the church has been found.
9. Is there any antagonism between the idea of personal religion and that of the social gospel?
10. Give some evidences of the barrenness of a materialistic life.

TOPICS FOR FURTHER STUDY

1. The idealism of the crusades.
2. A review of Rudolph Eucken's "Back to Religion."
3. Invisible powers in the inner life.
4. The idealism of the labor movement.
5. The church on the world's frontiers.

SUGGESTED READINGS

Finney, *Personal Religion and the Social Awakening*, particularly Chapters IV and V.

Jenks, *Social Significance of the Teachings of Jesus*, Study XI.

Mathews, *The Social Gospel*, Chapter XX.

Rauschenbusch, *Christianizing the Social Order*, Part 6, Chapter VI.

CHAPTER XIV

THE CHALLENGE TO THE CHURCH

"Never in human history were so many people, rich and poor, learned and ignorant, wise and otherwise, concerning themselves with social amelioration, dedicating themselves to philanthropy, organizing for industrial change, or applying the motives of religion to the problems of modern life." The passing of a score of years since Professor Peabody first penned these words has in no way lessened their truth. This interest is concerned with a situation in social life which constitutes a sharp challenge to the church. It is a situation which cannot be overlooked and a challenge which can by no means be ignored. This challenge to the church is evidenced, in the first place, by the present critical conditions. Consider these quotations from different writers in a single number of the Survey:

"Revolution is the vital fact of European politics to-day."

"At a time when the old 'Liberal' and 'Radical' and 'Progressive' parties of Europe have abdicated or been thrust aside, labor stands almost alone in its consciousness of large issues and insistent on its rightful share in deciding them."

"Unemployment is on the increase practically all over the United States, though the situation is not yet critical."

"Labor cannot longer be regarded as a commodity, like rubber or cheat, which can be stored on the shelf or in the bin in slack season for times of great demand."

These could be multiplied a hundred times and yet fall short of the whole truth. Human beings all about us are in dire need. The pressure of social maladjustment rests heavily, and most heavily upon those least able to bear it.

The three-fold challenge.—As danger is always a trumpet call to gallant souls, so human need is a challenge to the church. The Master said, "Come unto me, all ye that labor and are heavy laden, and I will give you rest." The church should interpret that message in terms of everyday life. If it is here to minister and not merely "theologize," it will seek to give this wonderful invitation to all who are burdened. It ought to be pretty clear that Jesus' way of bringing rest to men is through the ministry of his followers. Read again Matthew 25: 14–46 and Luke 9: 12–17. It is his power, but ministered through human hands. The charge is sometimes made that the church is more concerned with imposing a way of thinking upon men than it is with helping them in their life problems; more careful of dogma than of duty. Its surest answer to such a charge is in meeting this challenge of need with a program of help.

There could be, however, no hope of such an answer were it not for the second fact to be noticed as proof of the challenge. This fact is that the gospel does have a message of brotherhood and good will for just such times as these. The tree of life does indeed have leaves for the healing of the nations. What is to be said, however, of the church if, having the life-giving message, she shall fail to make it known? The very possession of such a priceless word imposes a trust and constitutes a challenge. In the preceding chapters the terms of this message have been examined in some detail and need not be restated now. It is a message of peace and hope, resting on the personal loyalty of individuals to Christ and functioning through their social living. It is a comprehensive message touching life at every point. The possession of such a word challenges the church as nothing else can.

Again the church is challenged by a very evident disposition to ignore it as a social agency. This distrust on the part of social leaders has been frequently expressed. At a meeting of social workers a certain piece of work was reported as "well done in spite of its having been done by the church." It is no uncommon thing for a group of working men to cheer the name of Christ and jeer at the church, which they feel fails to carry out his teachings.

Because of the moral quality of the social question, an intimate connection might be expected between the church and social progress; but, while such a connection does exist, it is by no means as close as it should be. The attitude of social workers toward the church varies all the way from violent opposition to cordial cooperation. Many view the church with distrust and agree with Pastor Nauman, who says, "Social democracy turns against Christ and the church because it sees in them only the means of providing religious foundation for the existing economic order." Or they feel with

Liebknecht that "Christianity is the religion of property and the respectable classes." Bebel goes even farther and regards both the church and Christianity as merely a passing phase. He says, "Christianity, then, the prevailing spiritual expression of the present economic order, must pass away as a better social order arrives." His social philosophy not only ignores Christianity, but offers a substitute for it. Professor Peabody sums up the situation with these words: "We find, then, a gulf of alienation and misinterpretation lying between the social movement and the Christian religion—a gulf so wide and deep as to recall the judgment of Schopenhauer that Christianity in its real attitude toward the world is absolutely remote from the spirit of the modern age. Yet, from the time when the social question began to take its present form, there have not failed to be heard a series of protests against this alienation of the new movement from the organization of the Christian life. To anyone, indeed, who has once recognized the ethical quality of the modern social question, the interpretation of it in terms of sheer philosophical materialism must appear a perversion of its characteristic aim, which can have occurred only through an unfortunate historical accident; what reason has the Christian Church for existing, many persons are now asking, if it is not to have a part in that shaping of a better world, which at the same time is the aim of the social movement?"[1]

The misunderstood church.—Then, too, it is difficult for us here in America to understand just

---

[1] *Jesus Christ and the Social Question*, p. 20. The Macmillan Company.

what the word "church" conveys to many foreign people of the working class. A report of the Federal Council of Churches of Christ in America makes this so clear that a portion of it may well be quoted here.

"The churches of America are not supported even in part by state funds, nor are they under state control. When one looks at government here, the church is not of necessity in the line of vision. There is no ecclesiastical factor in one's tax bill. Functionaries of a religious establishment do not sit, as such, in our Legislatures, and political vested rights do not control parochial policy. The churches are dependent upon the free will of the people, not upon the pleasure of the government, and policies of restraint or direction enacted into law and administered by the courts cannot be credited to or charged against the body of Christians as in the lands of established churches.

"This distinction, so familiar to American freemen, requires the constant renewal of emphasis, since no small part of the misunderstanding concerning the church's relation to industrial life in our country springs from the fact that multitudes born under the shadow of an ecclesiastical establishment, in this their new home impute to the American churches the power, the prejudices, and the defects of an ecclesiastical system here, by an impregnable constitutional provision, forever excluded."[2]

The man who has seen aristocratic misrule walking hand in hand with irreligious professional

---

[2] *The Church and Modern Industry*, a report adopted by the Federal Council in 1908.

ecclesiasticism finds it hard to understand our kind of a church or to believe that Christianity has anything for him. On the other hand, part of this estrangement must rest upon the members of the church. They have often been ignorant and uninterested in the problems of social welfare. There has not always been keenness of vision to see that a great historic struggle is going on. The importance of individual salvation has been so stressed in the teachings and evangelism of the past that it has been hard for some to realize that the gospel had any other message.

These individualists sometimes insist that the concern of the church is with salvation, and not with "soap and soup." They would limit all its activities to personal evangelism, with perhaps a little instruction along very conventional lines about the duty of righteous living. A selfish evangelistic appeal has been responsible for much of the lack of social vision in the church. Its message has been sounded in such phrases as: "Step over the line and be free," "Get into the ark of safety," "Get right with God," "Prepare for the other world." That the personal relationship between the individual and God must be right is fundamental, and there can be no departure from this great evangel. It is, however, equally fundamental that the saved individual must live a saved life; that heart changes shall find expression in social activities.

It must be confessed that the social ignorance of church members has frequently operated to widen this gulf. A well-known bishop, in a Lenten address some years ago, proclaimed himself a student of socialism and a friend of social progress. He then proceeded to give a definition of socialism which betrayed gross ignorance of its most fundamental propositions. Winston Churchill's picture of the church in *The Inside of the Cup* may be overdrawn and not true of any single church. It cannot be denied, on the other hand, that he has pointed out real faults and places of failure.

The value of criticism.—Now, however unjust we may feel some of these criticisms of the church to be, we cannot deny their existence, and that they indicate on the part of their authors an antagonistic attitude toward the church. However, criticism is never an unmixed evil. When just, it is to be taken in a spirit of humility as a stepping-stone toward correction and improvement. If, on the other hand, it lacks real foundation, it may at least indicate misunderstanding and lack of appreciation. This just as surely calls for some change of method that shall lead to understanding and appreciation. An unjust accusation may be most potent to provoke defense. If the church has a good record in social service, a vital, present interest, and a forward-looking purpose, then let her convince her critics by strong action. It is not the first time that circumstances have challenged the church, and we may have full faith that once again she will respond with the vigor and enthusiasm that shall compel final success.

The church's existence threatened.—There is still another aspect to this matter. The forces of evil are so strongly at work in the world that, unopposed, they threaten the very existence of Christian institutions themselves. The church is fighting for life. "This is the stake of the church in the social crises.

If one vast domain of life is dominated by principles antagonistic to the ethics of Christianity, it
will inculcate habits and generate ideas which will
undermine the law of Christ in all other domains of
life and even deny the theoretical validity of it. If
the church has not faith enough in its Christian law
to assert its sovereignty over all relations of society,
men will deny that it is a good and practical law
at all. If the church cannot conquer business,
business will conquer the church."[3]

These words of Professor Rauschenbusch were
written only fifteen years ago. In that short time
they have been fulfilled in part so startlingly as to
command our serious thought concerning the final
outcome. The line between the ideals of Christianity and those antagonistic to it are sharply
drawn. The church stands as always for unselfish
living and spiritual sensitiveness. Over against
that there are great organized sections of our business
world committed to selfish and materialistic gain;
there are other agencies frankly promoting amusement and pleasure as the *summum bonum;* there
are influential philosophies of life that are ego-
centric. It may not be true that the whole world
is "money-mad" and "pleasure-crazed," but those
phrases do characterize so large a section of society
as to give us pause. In the light of passing events
the church should clearly and promptly claim
sovereignty over all relations of society.

The verity of this challenge to the church lies
in the nature of the church. If it is but a human
institution expressing the longings of religious
instincts, a place for groping on toward God in a

[3] *Christianity and the Social Crisis*, pp. 341, 342.

blind sort of way, a workshop for forging out theolog-
ical theories, then the challenge will fall mostly on
deaf ears. If, however, the church is the repository
of divine truth, the guardian of God's message of
good-will toward men, a fortress for the forces of
righteousness, then, indeed, it will be a trumpet
call to battle. It need occasion no great surprise,
however, if history be repeated and some good
Christians fail to understand the challenge. The
same has been true in other emergencies. Sermons
were preached from Scripture texts in defense of
slavery. A united and aroused church could have
ended the temperance fight a decade ago. A movement so entirely along orthodox lines (though of
vast social significance also) as modern missions,
even now in the day of its success, wins but a tardy
and insufficient support from many. An outstanding duty of those who have caught this social vision
is to spread the message, to rouse the indifferent,
to educate the ignorant. As in all such crises, lack
of knowledge and apathy are the twin enemies
of progress. These must be overcome and the
challenge to the church made clear in the mind of
each of its faithful members. As the fiery cross
swept over Scotland, and set the most remote
clansman hurrying to Clan Alpine's aid, so may
there be a rallying to the support of the church and
its Master's cause.

EXERCISES

1. Do you think that more persons are applying
   motives of religion to the problems of modern
   life than ever before? Give reasons for your
   answer.

2. Give circumstances which you have noticed that indicate the present critical social condition.
3. What evidence do you see that church people are aware of the crisis and its challenge? Is such awareness increasing?
4. What did Jesus mean when he called his followers the salt of the earth?
5. Has the church had a preserving effect on communities?
6. Give an example of a social task which has been well done by the church.
7. Give an example of a failure to function socially by the church.
8. Why is the church often regarded as controlled by unsocial forces? Is it a just charge?
9. If the leadership of Jesus fails to change society, what hope do you see?
10. Compare the efficiency of the church with that of other social institutions.
11. Has the social viewpoint ever been presented in a Sunday-school class of which you were a member? If so, how?
12. Are the criticisms of the church for unsocial attitude deserved?

TOPICS FOR FURTHER STUDY

1. The social impulses in the gospel.
2. The reasons for distrust of the church by social workers.
3. The ethical content of socialism.
4. A review of *The Inside of the Cup*.
5. The stake of the church in the social crisis.

SUGGESTED READINGS

Mathews, *The Social Gospel*.

Peabody, *Jesus Christ and the Social Question*, Chapter I.

Rauschenbusch, *Christianizing the Social Order*, pp. 136–142.

CHAPTER XV

THE CHANCE OF THE CHURCH

Not only is the church meeting a challenge; it is offered a chance. If it will see the vision and accept the responsibility, the church may become leader in this great reconstruction period. The question of what to do is a very practical one, to which a variety of answers are being made. There is no lack of adverse criticism of the church for what it does or fails to do, but constructive suggestions are not so freely offered.

A four-fold program.—It would seem that a practical social program for the church might well include four main parts. First, there should be instruction about the essential facts of the social question. It should be impossible for anyone to grow up under the instruction of the Sunday school and church and remain in the crass ignorance of social facts which characterizes most church members to-day. This ignorance about such matters as housing, minimum wages, and child labor is a most serious indictment of our past methods of religious education. Such instruction may well be introduced as early as the Junior Department through illustrations and stories drawn from appropriate sources. A little later, when altruistic impulses are awaking, more detailed information may be given. The International Graded Lessons make

163

some provision through the course entitled "The World a Field for Service," in the later high-school years. In young people's and business men's classes more specific study can be undertaken. The purpose of such studies will be to present sufficient details to insure intelligent understanding, and especially to stimulate genuine interest in the many-sided social question.

With this should go a study of the social significance of the gospel. A physician who knew all the symptoms of his "case," but had no knowledge of the remedies to apply, could render his patient little service. Here, again, the appropriate method is to make a social approach whenever the regular Sunday-school lessons permit, and to undertake more detailed study later.

The following list of available helps and books is not at all complete, but does serve to indicate some of the material which has been prepared for these two lines of instruction: For a general presentation of the social question, the first and fourth years of the Senior Graded Lessons, *The Social Principles of Jesus*, by Rauschenbusch, and *The Social Gospel*, by Mathews. For a general view and more detailed study of certain problems, "The Gospel of the Kingdom," a series edited by Dr. Josiah Strong. For a more direct examination of the teachings themselves may be added *The Social Significance of the Teachings of Jesus*, by Jenks; Peabody's *Jesus Christ and the Social Question*, and Mathews' *Social Teachings of Jesus*. The list of books and courses dealing with specific problems is a long one, and includes child labor, immigration, the city, housing, and many other topics. The selection of a text for a given class will, of course, depend upon the age and previous study along social lines of its members. Usually the specific study of problems mav well be preceded by a more general course.

In the third place, provision must be made for direct cooperation at some point. What form this will take depends somewhat upon the location of the church and the surrounding community. It should establish a contact between workers in the church and some of the immediate problems. This participation is necessary, because it furnishes a sort of laboratory. Vital contact with urgent needs helps to lift interest off the plane of the academic and perfunctory. Again, such participation is necessary, because in some fields the church alone can render a disinterested service. The officers of a municipal league may be suspected (even though unjustly) of furthering their own political interests. The pressure brought to bear on Legislatures is well known. Comparatively, the church as an organization is untrammeled. Such direct help is also a guarantee of good faith. It is one thing to study quietly or even get quite indignant over conditions; it is quite another to get out and fight the abuse. The full measure of the church's action has rather frequently been to pass resolutions which some one has called "empty blusterings at an absent foe." When the sincerity of Christian interest is questioned, no argument is quite so convincing as some constructive effort to render substantial aid.

A good many Christian people have been pretty slow to see the chance of the church in such service. They prefer to keep goodness in general terms and are timid when it comes to specific applications. They like to do all their religious thinking in terms of ancient times. Their interest in Joseph and the famine in Egypt is keen and perennial, but they can conceive no reason for the church being concerned with the underfed multitudes of to-day. Christ's words to the sinning woman whose accusers went out one by one while he wrote in the sand, have no possible connection in their minds with the white-slave traffic of America's cities.

Finally, the church's greatest chance is that of inspiring leadership. The answer to the charge that Christianity has failed is that, on the contrary, it is the only thing that has succeeded. Some say that it is impotent and point to the failure of the church at times. They forget that that is a failure of men to interpret and live out the principles of Christianity, and not an evidence of the failure of those principles. Freely admitting all the slowness and lack of vision on the part of church members, and remembering all the times when cause has been given for criticism, it still remains true that the church has been a great socializing agency. As Doctor Bogardus says, "The dynamic of Christianity has operated not only through the high ideals which it furnishes, . . . but also through the social service which its exponents have rendered."[1] Statistics collected by Mr. Stelzle show that 92 per cent of associated charity workers, 88 per cent of social settlement workers, and 71 per cent of general social workers were church members. These percentages were found among more than a thousand

---

[1] *Introduction to Sociology*, p. 252.

workers, and may be assumed to indicate that most social workers have gained at least a portion of their vision from the church.

Among the institutions of our civilization two stand out preeminently in which the social welfare has been preserved against the attacks of selfishness. These are the home and the school. Both of these owe their present position, in a large degree, to the church. The sacredness of the family has been consistently maintained in the teaching of the church. Marriage has been held sacred by the church, even in the minds of many for whom it constitutes the sole remaining bond with anything religious. The Christian character of the family has been so successfully defended that it remains the one institution of human life which, with any appropriateness, may be used as a figure of the ideal relation between God and men, and between man and man.

So in the case of education, it has been the church which, particularly in the latter days, supplied the ideals and frequently the material means as well. Many a great college had its inception in the faith and labors and sacrifices of some group of Christian men. When aggressive interests pushed the frontiers of early colonization in this country further and further West, it was the churches which stood for the higher interests of man's need. Side by side stood the rude chapel and the log schoolhouse. Indeed, one building frequently served for both purposes, and the teacher's desk became on Sunday the preacher's pulpit. Academies were founded, colleges started, and the young people urged to make use of them.

Another example of the socializing activities of the organized church is found in its missionary efforts. The men and women who with unselfish fervor have penetrated the dark corners of the earth have wrought a marvelous transformation in the life conditions of India, China, Africa, and the islands of the sea. They have overcome superstition, planted hospitals, built industries, created literature, invented written languages, changed customs, and been true messengers of the gospel of transformed life as the inevitable result of accepting the good news of Jesus Christ.

It is not too much to say that the growth of altruism through the centuries has been mainly due to the constant insistence by the church on the ideals of Jesus. It may often have been slow to make the specific applications to its own age that it should. We have a way of spending more sympathy on the sorrows of Israel under Egyptian taskmasters than those of men in our own factories. But nevertheless the ages would have been very dark but for the social message brought by the church.

Idealism the creative task of the church.—The great task of the church will ever be to give ideals. It will continue to be the great recruiting station for the army of social workers. It is in the church that men and women are most effectively introduced to Christ, in whose spirit they go forth for service to their fellows. Men have been imbued with many motives in the fellowship of the church, such as zeal for the truth, devotion to doctrine, interest in the organization; but the finest motive they have found there is the impulse to unselfish service. Thus the most noble service of the church will be to lift the whole movement of social reconstruction on to a higher plane. Most of the social philosophies and plans of reform have put a strong emphasis on the need of justice in such matters as wages, taxes, hours of labor, and the like. These are the points at which social injustice and maladjustment are evident, and it is therefore quite natural that a good deal of attention should be paid to corrective measures. There is, however, danger that attention will be paid too exclusively to these material affairs. It is very probable that the adoption of some of the plans proposed would indeed result in improvement. There is no assurance, however, that the reconstructed society would not be still grossly materialistic. Every one of these plans depends for its ultimate success on the qualities of brotherliness and unselfishness, but provides no means of inculcating these virtues in men's hearts. That is the contribution of supreme value that Jesus makes. He not only aims at social improvement, but so grips the lives of men that they are enabled to come up to his high ideals of life.

The basic principle of the social gospel is found in these words of Jesus: "Whosoever wishes to save his life will lose it, and whoever, for my sake and my gospel's, loses his life shall find it." He is talking here not of martyrdom, but of service. It is the application to the lives of his followers of his own rule of life: "For their sakes I sanctify myself." The key to all acts of life under this rule is found in those other words of his: "Thou shalt love thy neighbor as thou dost thyself." And a final success is assured in these words of encouragement, "Fear not, little flock, for it is your Father's good will to give you the kingdom."

EXERCISES

1. Is the church a valuable social agency?
2. How do local churches vary in their attitude toward social service?   Why?
3. What connection is there between such institutions as the Y. M. C. A., Red Cross, and rescue missions as social agents and the church?
4. Does the church have a social responsibility?
5. Why do nonreligious people wish to be married by clergymen?
6. Explain: The family is the most appropriate figure of the relation between God and man.
7. Show how the church has maintained man's highest interests on civilization's frontiers.
8. Name five social results of foreign missions.
9. Mention some hindrances to the growth of social vision in the church.
10. What are some of the dynamics of social action?
11. How would you bring social ideas to a class of fifteen-year-old boys?   Contrast the social work of a church in a residence district with one in a foreign population.
12. How can the rural church serve its community?

TOPICS FOR FURTHER STUDY

1. The proper relation between the church and the various specific social agencies.
2. The Y. M. C. A., Red Cross, and rescue mission,

considered as the *church* specializing in social service.

3. Foreign missions—a socializing force.
4. Religion as the dynamic of social work.
5. The accomplishments of the church in social service.
6. A program of social activities for the Sunday school.

SUGGESTED READINGS

Mathews, *The Social Gospel*, Chapter XVIII.

Rauschenbusch, *Christianity and the Social Crisis*, pp. 319-324, 329-342.

Report of the Federal Council of the Churches of Christ in America, *The Church and Modern Industry*. (December, 1908.)

Ward, *The Social Creed of the Churches*.

BIBLIOGRAPHY

The following books are suggested as a basis for a reference library. Many other titles might well be added, especially in the definite field covered in Part Two. Some of these will be found in the "Suggested Readings" following each chapter. It is very desirable, of course, that the entire list should be available, but if this is not possible, the first seven are the ones most frequently referred to:

Mathews. *The Social Gospel*, The American Baptist Publication Society, Philadelphia.

Rauschenbusch. *Christianizing the Social Order*, The Macmillan Company, New York.

Peabody. *Jesus Christ and the Social Question*, The Macmillan Company, New York.

Weymouth. *New Testament in Modern Speech*, The Pilgrim Press, Boston.

Finney. *Personal Religion and the Social Awakening*, The Abingdon Press, New York.

Batten. *The Social Task of Christianity*, Fleming H. Revell Company, Chicago.

Whitaker. *The Gospel at Work in Modern Life*, American Baptist Publication Society, Philadelphia.

Jenks. *Political and Social Significance of Life and Teachings of Jesus*, Association Press, New York.

Rauschenbusch. *Christianity and the Social Crisis*, The Macmillan Company, New York.

Rauschenbusch. *The Social Principles of Jesus*, Association Press, New York.

Stelzle. *American Social and Religious Conditions*, Fleming H. Revell Company, Chicago.

Ward. *The Social Creed of the Churches*, The Abingdon Press, New York.

Taylor. *Religion in Social Action*. Dodd, Mead & Company, New York.

Kent. *The Social Teachings of the Prophets and Jesus*, Charles Scribner's Sons, New York.

Bogardus. *Introduction to Sociology*, The University of Southern California Press, Los Angeles.

Addams. *Democracy and Social Ethics*, The Macmillan Company, New York.

Ward. *The Social Center*, D. Appleton & Company, New York.

www.ingramcontent.com/pod-product-compliance
Lightning Source LLC
Chambersburg PA
CBHW060308100426
42812CB00003B/705